The Living
Kain

The Living Thoughts of
Kant

Julien Benda

Rupa & Co

Copyright © Rupa & Co., 2002

Published 2002 by
Rupa & Co
7/16, Ansari Road, Daryaganj,
New Delhi 110 002

Sales Centres:

Allahabad Bangalore Chandigarh Chennai
Dehradun Hyderabad Jaipur Kathmandu
Kolkata Ludhiana Mumbai Pune

All rights reserved.
No part of this publication may be reproduced, stored in a retrieval system, or transmitted, in any form or by any means, electronic, mechanical, photocopying, recording or otherwise, without the prior permission of the publishers.

ISBN 81-7167-863-7

Typeset 11 pts. Zapf Elliptical by
Nikita Overseas Pvt Ltd,
1410 Chiranjiv Tower,
43 Nehru Place
New Delhi 110 019

Printed in India by
Gopsons Papers Ltd.
A-14 Sector 60
Noida 201 301

Contents

Kant	1
Critique of Pure Reason	48
Fundamental Principles of the Metaphysic of Morals	132
Critique of Practical Reason	136
Religion within the Limits of Reason alone	199
Critique of Judgment	205

The Works of Immanuel Kant

(1724-1804)

Universal History of Nature (1755)
Monadologia Physica (1756)
Dreams of a Spirit-Seer (1761)
The Sole Basis for the Existence of God (1763)
Observations on the Sentiment of the Beautiful and the Sublime (1764)
Dissertation on the Principles of the Sensible and the Intelligible Word (Inaugural Dissertation) (1770)
Critique of Pure Reason (1781)
Prolegomena to Any Future Metaphysics (1783)
Idea of a Universal History on a Cosmo-Political Plan (1784)

Fundamental Principles of the Metaphysic of Morals (1785)
Conjectures on the Beginnings of the History of the Human Race (1786)
Critique of Practical Reason (1788)
Critique of Judgement (1790)
Religion within the Limits of Reason Alone (1793)
Perpetual Peace (1795)
Metaphysic of Morals (1796-1797)
Philosophy of Law (1797)
Principles of Virtue (1797)
Anthropology (1799)

Kant

I

It is a common saying that philosophers' lives consist of little more than biographies of their ideas. And indeed the essentially meditative nature of that breed of men seems to exclude from their careers, as though by necessity, those adventures and revolutions or at least such adventures and revolutions as are deliberate, so frequently encountered in the lives of poets and novelists. It is hard to call to mind any philosopher whose life could be made into a movie, as could the lives of a Torquato Tasso, a Byron. Yet it is equally true that, since philosophers are not, however much they may nobly wish it, pure intellects, operating independently of their environments, certain fortuitotus circumstances of their existence can, at least to some extent, have determined their ideas. Thus also other circumstances, not fortuitous but actually desired, and also certain of the philosophers' own actions, can explain some aspect of their moral make-up, such as will later appear in their philosophy. Thus men have tried to see in the youthful Descartes's choice of the profession of arms a correspondence with the essentially bold quality of his philosophy, or in Spinoza's refusal of inherited riches a correspondence with the stocism of his teachings.[1] It follows, then, that from one point of view knowledge of the lives of philosophers is not altogether without value in interpreting their thought. This seems to me to be the case with the master with whom we are here concerned.

Immanuel Kant was born at Koenigsberg (Prussia) on April 22, 1724. Some have seen significance in the fact that his father was of Scottish descent and have thought that this accounted for the thinkers of that country. It seems to me less far fetched to attach importance to the pietistic atmosphere in which the young Kant was brought up by his parents—a pietism which constituted a reaction against dogmatic Protestantism, a pietism which valued exaltation of the spirit, confidence in good intention, *fromme Gesinnung*, more than theological science—and to ask whether this does not show a correspondence with the rôle which this kind of religion will play in the philosopher's thinking. It is less far fetched to realize that his mother, Anne Reuter, who would seem to have exerted upon him a very special influence, strove to make him share her feeling for nature, and to associate this fact with

---

1. Cf. No. 7: *The Living Thoughts of Spinoza* presented by Arnold Zweig.

he attempt which he will later make to combine his religious belief with his admiration at cosmic phenomena; to observe that while he was a student at the University of Koenigsberg he showed a marked preference for Latin studies, because the Romans made cult of duty and discipline, and that he continually quoted these lines of Juvenal:

Summum crede nefas animam proeferre pudori
Et propter vitam vivendi predere causas.
(Consider it the worst of iniquities to subject one's spirit to shame and for the sake of life to lose the reasons for living.)

From the age of twenty-one and over a period of ten years Kant acted as tutor in families of the East Prussian nobility (the Hülsens, the kayserlings); granted that he thus acquired a certain knowledge of the world and also of that morality which Nietzsche later dubbed the "master morality"[2] and against which the author of the *Critique of Practical Reason* was to react so forcibly, still, if one can judge by the fact that a number of his former pupils were the first to abolish serfdom on their estates, it would seem that his teaching already included that respect for man as man which was to be the basis of his ethics. After his return to Koenigsberg in 1755 he was made a *Privatdozent*; then, in 1770, a professor of philosophy; in 1780, a

---

2. Cf. No. 5: *The Living Thoughts of Nietzsche* presented by Heinrich Mann.

member of the academic Senate; in 1786, rector of the University. From then on his life consisted entirely in fulfilling his academic duties and in working at his writings. One can discover meaning in his remaining celibate, seemingly on principle, if one considers that fact in relation to the passages in his *Philosophy of Law* where, discussing marriage, he sees therein only a contract between two people in love, and seems not to be aware of the compatibility of marriage with a more spiritual union. It is a testimony to the punctilious regularity of his habits of life that, according to a widely circulated story, his neighbours were astounded one day—he had just received a copy of Rousseau's *Emile*[3]—when he was not seen taking his daily constitutional. Yet political events interested him deeply; first the American Revolution, then the French aroused his enthusiasm. Once fame had touched him (and from far lands men made pilgrimages to Koenigsberg to catch a glimpse of him), how did he conduct himself? Probably he agreed with the saying of Spinoza: "Gloria non est virtus sed de virtute oriri potest. (There is no virtue in fame, but fame can arise from virtue.)" His last years were saddened by the attacks directed by the government of Prussia's new king, Frederick William II, a superstitious and intolerant monarch, against his book, *Religion within the Limits of Reason Alone*; such attacks he answered along the line of a sentence found in his personal papers: "The king can

---

3. Cf. No. 9: *The Living Thoughts of Rousseau* presented by Romain Rolland.

determine my earthly fate, but he cannot force me to deny my conscience and my inner convictions." Still we shall see that his devotion to liberty did not extend so far as to admit the right of rebellion. Kant died at Koenigsberg on February 12, 1804, after a period of sterile senility and a lingering illness.

The fact that Kant was a professor of philosophy leads me to point out a distinction, which in itself deserves study, between philosophers who engaged in teaching and those who were purely solitary spirits, men of whom Spinoza is the prototype. It may be granted that if the writings of the latter, directed at the expression of the author's thought, as it were for himself alone and with very little idea of gaining followers, are for that very reason more condensed, more strictly ordered, more artistic, the work of the former is more social, better calculated to affect humanity as a whole—a thing which explains why such work involves repetitions, an over abundance of proofs, a certain lack of order which makes it more living. Add to that the fact that Kant, as his contemporaries bear witness, sought to adapt his teaching to the comprehension of the multitude and to instruct those who listened to him, not in philosophy—the existence of which, in the then nature of things, he denied—but to philosophize. There again we find in his day-to-day activities things characteristic of his teachings: the idea that truth is not the exclusive property of a few privileged spirits but is open to all, and the banishment of dogmatism.[4]

---

4. In 1799 the *Magasin encyclopédique* published a translation of a letter dealing with Kant which had appeared in the *Jahrbücher*

6   KANT

It would seem that Kant's attempt to develop a system of thought accessible to the mass of men has, as might have been expected, proved a failure. We know that it was because he saw that his *Critique of Pure Reason* found so

---

der preussischen Monarchie. It is described by A. Aulard, who quotes this letter in his introduction to Kant's political works, as a kind of interview. Its writer saw "...a thin little man, very stooped, whose eyes, like all the rest of his features, create a disagreeable impression..." But his conversation is pleasant and voluble. "What he most likes to discuss are things which relate to physical geography and to politics; indeed political affairs are generally speaking his favourite study, or rather recreation. He occupies a great part of his leisure time with the reading of gazettes and other periodicals. It is extremely interesting to listen to his opinions on such matters; for many a circumstance which you would consider of little import assumes very great significance in his view, by consequences of his keen observation. He discovers many a cause, which would never have occurred to you, for events that have taken place and points to future consequences, which have already only too often been justified. But what is principally noteworthy are his observations, descriptions and accounts of every sort of matter relating to geography and especially to physical geography. In spite of his never having gone further than two or three miles from his native Koenigsberg, he is so well acquainted with each country's location, climate, government, economy, and even its provinces, districts and towns, the character, manners and customs of its inhabitants, that they tell a story of how one day a traveller, freshly returned from China and hearing him discourse in company on that contry, asked him how long it was since he had returned form it. Indeed seeing him in company, one would never believe that this charming and merry fellow could be the author of that profound work, the *Critique of Pure Reason*."

few readers that he wrote his *Prolegomena to Any Future Metaphysics*, a book which he believed set forth in easy form the ideas of the *Critique* and which he intended for the public, the general public. Here is a specimen of the touching simplicity characteristic of certain great minds: the belief that truth in its own right should interest men, and that they will quite naturally make the effort required to grasp it. And furthermore that abstract thought, because it is their own daily bread, is the common food of all their fellows.

II

Kant's philosophic enquiries were principally concerned with four questions: the mechanics of knowing; ethics; religion; and finally the nature of aesthetic feeling and the direction of biological evolution. On each of these questions he expressed ideas which marked decisive turning points in the history of human thought.

In so far as the nature of knowing is concerned, Kant's importance lies less in results of his studies, however important they may be, than in the fact that he proposed the question. Before him, with the exception of certain British thinkers, to whom indeed he was to acknowledge his debt, philosophers constructed their systems upon concepts of which they had subjected to examination neither the origin nor the limits within which the employment of such concepts was admissible. This was true of Descartes, of Spinoza, of Malebranche, of Leibniz, of the scholastic, of the philosophers of classical antiquity. It occurred to Kant to consider the problem of how these concepts had come into being and to what extent it was proper to make use of them. In other words, he was the first to think of studying the nature of human understanding before taking into account its fruits. Our philosopher did not arrive at any such notion, at least in any formal sense, fresh out of the bag, but rather through a process whose course can be examined. His first concern was to set up a basis for his religious ideas, and he thought that he saw such a basis in the concatenation of natural phenomena, which he would have determined the one by the other, rather than subject to chance (*Universal History of Nature*, 1755; *Monadologia Physica*, 1756; *The Sole Basis for the Existence of God*, 1763); thus he is led to consider the origin of the concept of causality and, in general, the nature of our processes of thought. At this stage it seemed to him that this process pre-eminently consisted in comparison and in analysis, and that the error of the philosophers who had preceded him lay in their building with insufficiently analysed materials—of which he principally objected to the concept of the intelligence. Thus in his *Dreams of a Spirit-Seer* (1761) he pokes fun at the ease with which it is possible to build up a system of spiritualism (for example, that of Swedenborg) if only one sets up as a basic principle, outside the possibility of criticism, the concept of a spiritual substance. A few years later, probably in 1769, which he signalized as a year of major importance in his intellectual evolution, he experienced what he later called, in attributing it to the influence of Hume, "the awakening from his dogmatic slumbers," dogmatism being defined as "the presumption of wishing to make progress only through a pure intellect, founded upon concepts in accordance with principles such as have long been used by the reason, without examination of how and by what right the reason came to their use." This attitude is more and more strongly asserted over the years that follow, as is evidenced in his famous *Dissertation on the Principles of the Sensible and the Intelligible World* (1770) and in the philosopher's letters and notes. At last it was fully to burst forth in his major work—the *Critique of Pure Reason* (1781).

The central idea of this book seems to me already to have been stated with all the clarity one can desire in this passage from the *Dissertation*: "I found that many of the principles which we consider objective are in reality subjective, that is to say they involve only those conditions under which we conceive or understand the object." Furthermore Kant's position in neatly defined by means of the celebrated comparison he makes between his discovery and that of Copernicus. Just as it is the frame of reference within which we live as dwellers on the earth which leads to the heavens seeming to revolve around us so, he points out, it is the nature of our process of knowing which leads things to appear to us under the aspect of space and of time. In other words, space and time instead of being attributes inherent in the objects of our knowledge are element of that knowing itself, considered independently of its objects. Space and time are what Kant was to call *forms*, as distinguished from the *matter* of our cognition, in the latter of which objects actually have their being. Or again space and time are *pure intuitions* and not general concepts hemming in the relations between things. Or again they are *a priori* data of our process of knowing, even though we know them only as a result of experience. It is upon this that Kant based what he was to call his *transcendental philosophy*, a term which relates not to objects but to our way of knowing them.[5] The celebrated criticisms produced by this union of time and space under a single head are well known—among others that of Bergson, for whom psychological time, which he calls "duration," and which would be truly a form of our process of knowing, is completely unconnected with space, especially with that fundamental attribute which is mensurability. (Of course it remains a question whether mensurable time, "spatial" time, is not a form of cognition. Then too, Kant, in his *Transcendental Logic*, sets up a difference between time and space, and even a certain subordination of the latter to the former.) Also well known are the objections taken to his conception of space, notably on the part of mathematical philosophers like Louis Couturat and Henri Poincaré.[6] It is no less true that in confining space within the operation of the mind, Kant wrecked the philosophical systems which incline to

---

5. "I call transcendental the principle which embodies the general *a priori* condition under which alone things can become the object of our congnition in general." (*Critique of Aesthetic Judgment*, Introduction, V.)
6. On this point see *Revue des Cours et Conférences*, April 4, 1895.

explain the process of knowing by spatial devices independent of that process. And above all is it true that, however subject to criticism his findings may be, it was he who set for philosophy—at least in an imperative way—that entirely new problem of the nature of cognition, a problem which was to give rise to such works as the *Basis of Induction* by Lacelier, the *Psychology* of Renouvier, the *Essay on the Principal Elements of Representations* by Hamelin, *The Immediate Data of Consciousness* by Bergson. It can be said that Kant originated the study of the human consciousness. That achievement alone would suffice to make secure his fame.

The basic idea of the *Critique of Pure Reason* astonishes at once by the fact that it is logical and self-evident and by the fact that its advent comes at so late a date in the intellectual history of mankind. How is it possible that it should have taken men thirty centuries to realize that a criticism of the reasoning process is the necessary prerequisite for any possible truths which have the reason as their basis? That is the sort of question one asks when confronted with many a discovery of genius; but it seems as though this time it were possible to give an answer. The first activity of thinking man was to make use of his faculties and to enjoy their fruits. The earliest of the Greek thinkers, according to Abel Rey in his *Youth of Greek Science*, were "intoxicated by the reason." To criticize its powers implies a certain detachment from their results, a certain asceticism, and could only take place in an altogether adult state of humanity. Criticism was born in our time, says Ernest Renan at the outset of his *Studie in*

Religious History; he could have added that it would have been difficult for it to have been born earlier. Once unleashed by the work of Kant, criticism of the reason was to produce a movement which flowered forth in the succeeding ages and which consists in examining the relations between the reason and the particular sciences to which it claims to apply. Thus with Renan this movement questions to what extent the reason is capable of grasping historical reality; with Bergson it thinks that this faculty, marvellously adapted to knowledge of physical phenomena, is far less so to the knowledge of psychological and biological matters; with Poincaré, it states that Euclidean geometry is not especially conformable to the reason, but is simply more convenient than any other. The *Critique of Pure Reason* initiated what one might call the trial of the reason.

At the same time as Kant subjected to scrutiny the concepts of space and time, he subjected to scrutiny the greater part of our fundamental concepts (substance, causality, reciprocal action) and made every effort to reduce them to a minimum. The schema of twelve categories which he drew up for his purpose, categories[7] on which all others would be dependent, is a specimen of those results to which a philosopher, by a common aberration, attaches capital importance, whereas posterity, apart from the learned, scarcely remembers them. On the

---

7. Cf. D. Parodi, "The Critique of the Kantian Categories," *Revue de Métaphysique et de Morale*, 1904.

other hand, in the course of this study Kant happened upon an idea to which he seems to have assigned less value than he did to his twelve categories, and yet which we considerably esteem. Giving special attention to those concepts which express a relation, he finds that a relation can occour not only through comparison but by connection, and comes to the conclusion that the striving after connection, and more generally the faculty of synthesis (the unifying faculty) which is at the same time the master faculty, is the basic condition for the operations of the consciousness—an idea which, although opposed by the associationists, particularly by the pluralism of William James and by a recent school (Léon Brunschvicg), according to which the need for unity is only a temporary need of the mind destined to be superseded, remains all the same for most thinkers, and, I believe, rightly and expression of truth.

If to *pure intuitions* (space and time) and to *forms of the understanding*, of which the principal one is, then, the unifying faculty,[8] we add *transcendental ideas* (idea of the soul, idea of the world, idea of God), we have the whole of the a *priori* forms without which those data could not be thought. Here is the essence of the *Critique of Pure Reason*.

We shall not here concern ourselves at length (we shall come back to it when we take up the question of

---

8. The forms of the understanding differ from pure intuitions in that they are essentially *active*, while the latter are, according to Kant, above all *receptive*.

Kantian free will) with the famous problem of the *thing-in-itself*, the question which Kant raises over knowing whether things possess intrinsic existence, independent of the knowledge we have of them through the forms of our cognition and the categories of our understanding; or, to use his own terms, whether the *noumenon* exists independently of the *phenomenon*. Kant always asserted that he believed in the thing-in-itself. Thus it has been pointed out, with reference to that chapter in the *Transcendental Analytic* entitled "On the Basis of the Division of All Things in General into Phenomena and Nounmena," that, in contrast to Plato, for whom phenomena have their being just as much as noumena, for Kant noumena alone have being, while phenomena are merely the appearances furnished us by things, reflected by our mental make-up. Moreover he sharply opposes his *transcendental idealism*, which assumes the existence of the thing-in-itself, to that which assumes the existence of the thing-in-itself, to that which he scornfully calls *transcendental realism*, wherein time, space and the material object contained therein would be realities. Nevertheless one has the feeling that his critic, Jacobi, is right when he maintains that logically Kant should have denied all existence apart from our perceptions and should have professed a pure, subjective idealism such as, I might add, that called absolute subjectivism, which Fichte ascribed to the Kantian doctrine as its natural interpretation, and the language of which is made his own by the author of *Pure Reason* when he writes, "Phenomena exist in space and space exists in me." Or better still, he should have professed the idealism propounded by John Stuart Mill when he considers the external world as simply a "possibility for perceptions." Such reflections would lead us to think that with Kant, belief in the thing-in-itself was much more a result of his religious education than of a conviction founded upon reasoning. Then, too on this subject his statements have always somewhat seemed to lack precision; thus he speaks of the reasons which *lead to belief* in the thing-in-itself; concerning its nature, he asserts (*Prolegomena*, Part Two, No. 32) that "we do not know, we cannot know anything whatever which is determinate." Here more than anywhere else he is resolved to substitute, following his celebrated formula, *belief* for *knowledge* (*Glauben* for *Wissen*). In short, the question of the existence of the thing-in-itself (or of the reality of the external world, for it comes to the same thing), after Kant as before Kant, remains, whatever may be said about it, a question of personal preference on the metaphysical, or, more precisely, the religious, level, and not a scientific question. Our philosopher's distinction perhaps lies precisely in his having had a presentiment of the non-scientific character of the problem, and having thus helped to free rational philosophy of it, as the nineteenth century was expressly to do. But we cannot say that in this he set the human mind a new problem, as he did in seeking to find the conditions of our cognition.

What seems to me, on the other hand, of major importance is Kant's work in pointing out that the concepts of our minds, having been moulded within the limits set by experience, are illegitimately used when we apply them, as has the generality of philosophers, to objects which are essentially outside these limits: the existence of God, the reality of a spiritual substance, the beginning of the world, freedom of the will, immortality.[9] It seems to me that in this Kant brought about a revolution which again can be related (he himself compared his work to that of Copernicus) to a revolution which has taken place in science: the revolution by virtue of which modern physics has declared that there is no reason to believe that the laws of classical mechanics, discovered through the study of phenomena, are equally valid for atomic phenomena.[10] It is well known how Kant set out to demonstrate this illegitimate use of our concepts. He describes as *synthetic a priori judgments* those used in

---

9. Kant illustrated this idea with a very happy metaphor. The same thing happens, he says, to a mind which ventures outside the limits of experience as would happen to a dove if it were to imagine that, because it can easily fly through air, it could with equal ease fly through space. Elsewhere, wishing to show (*Transcendental Dialectic*, II, III, 5) the mystery for the human reason which is necessarily in every being, even in God, he represents Him as saying to Himself: "From one eternity to another I am; nothing exists apart from Me except by My will; but from whence then am I?" Clearly our author is one of those in whom an ability to make abstractions does not exclude the gift of striking imagery.
10. Cf. Maurice de Broglie, *Atomes, radioactivités, transmutations*, p. 70.

mathematics and physics—*synthethic* because they unite terms not necessarily implied one by the other; *a priori* in that they are stated before they are in any way experienced and because they admit of necessity and universality. He insists that this kind of judgment is not valid for metaphysics, even though constantly used therein, because here the reason is not concerned, as it is in mathematics and physics, with phenomena which always continue to be possible subjects of experience. As illustration of his thesis, he points out the contradictions into which the reason falls when it undertakes to solve through these concepts the problems to which I have referred. These are his celebrated *antinomies*, which consist in showing that by the use of these concepts, especially the concepts of quantity and causality, one can reach solutions of these problems which are diametrically opposed to each other and yet equally valid from the point of view of the reason. Thus one can demonstrate equally well that the world must have a beginning in time and boundaries in space, or else that it is limitless in both; that matter both is and is not indefinitely divisible; that the concatenation of phenomena arises from a first cause, or that such a cause is inconceivable. So also he shows how weak, in the light of pure reason, are the classical proofs of the existence of God, Who is for him merely an *ideal of cognition*, possessing for Kant the moralist, however, sovereign importance. The many criticisms directed against these conclusions of Kant are widely known, especially those directed against his assertions regarding *synthetic a priori judgments*, the existence of which has been denied; his antinomies, of which it has been thought possible to establish (Renouvier) that they do not possess equal validity for the reason, or else that, as between the *thesis* and the *antithesis*, Kant in fact prefers the antithesis, while insisting that he prefers neither. Yet it remains true that Kant in peremptory fashion called upon the human mind to distinguish between that which stems from experience and that which, unrelated to experience (the "unknowable" of Auguste Comte and Herbert Spencer) pertains to faith, even though, in his view, as we shall see later, faith lies within the realm of the reason.

It seems to me that Kant likewise did the human mind a great service by setting up the idea of the reason independent of experience (even though the reason only knows itself through experience) and by objecting before the event to those modern systems which would have us believe that the reason is in no way immutable, that the reason is the bondservant of experience and could well change if the latter should some day come to require it. Such views seem baffling when we consider that (1) the whole history of science, from the Greeks to the present day, consists in the reason emerging finally victorious and perfectly self-consistent from every situation in which experience called upon it to abdicate, or at least to change its nature (I am thinking of the explanation which the reason finally gave to the problem of the "irrational" number, of the "imaginary" quantity; need I point out that the reason remains wholly unscathed by the "determinism" of the new physics?); and that (2) the reason is no longer in any sense moulded by experience but is now pre-existent to experience, that it is the reason which interprets experience, so that if experience thought it could demonstrate the failure of the reason in the form in which we make use of the reason, experience would do so by using the reason itself, and would by that very fact spoil its own demonstration. And I am not forgetting that during distant ages of the earth's history, when man was struggling against his environment and erecting the foundations of his nature, the reason arose from experience, from the advantages which the reason produced. But today the reason forgets this humble origin and considers itself transcendental in relation to the circumstances under which it is employed. How could one praise too highly the man who came to remind his fellows that they possess a faculty henceforward immutable, and by the same token almost divine, above the ever-changing and uncertain world of their perceptions?[11]

III

As we now proceed to that part of Kant's thought which concerns moral problems, that thought seems particularly to evoke a distinction which applies to the ideas of most philosophers. In general it is

---

11. One can "learn" absolutely nothing from experience, as A. Lange well put it in his commentary on Kant (*History of Materialism*, II, p. 52), if one has not been so constituted by nature as to enable one to connect subject and attribute, cause and effect.

possible to consider the ideas of a philosopher from two points of view. One can consider them in relation to the philosopher himself, and, to a degree, in relation to himself alone. This involves tracing the development of an idea in a specific mind, taking into account all the problem which have engaged a philosopher's attention, without concerning ourselves over the extent of their real importance, and considering them worthy of study merely by virtue of the fact that they captured his attention. Such a study basically belongs as much to individual psychology as to philosophy. When the individual who serves as its object is a great thinker, it can teach us profound lesson. On the other hand one can consider the ideas of a philosopher in relation to mankind; that is to say to the extent that they have been remembered by groups of men, have unsettled their former conceptions, have become points of departure for other, entirely new conceptions. This second kind of study belongs rather to what one could call the social history of ideas. It does not at all necessarily duplicate the first method of approach. For, although it is possible to say that the ideas which mankind has remembered in the work of a philosopher are generally the ideas to which he himself attached importance, still it remains true that many of the problems which have greatly preoccupied him, as well as the solutions he found for them, have become of little interest to posterity (we have already seen a specimen of this in Kant's *categories*) and concern only specialists in the subject. Let us examine Kant's ethical works successively from each point of view.

Kant's ethical speculations arise, like his theory of congnition, from his reaction against the dogmatists and their undertaking to build with materials which have not been subjected to criticism. Under the influence of Rousseau, and breaking with the philosophers of the enlightenment, Kant reached this conviction (1762): that man's worth does not lie only in the light of his intelligence, but rather and above all in feeling, in the intimacy and depth of the soul; and he embraces and idea which he will never abandon, and which will serve as one of the bases of his teaching: the idea of the dignity of man to the extent that man is a being endowed with personality, of the dignity of the *human person*. He has himself indicated how much he owed to his reading of Rousseau: "I was," he says, "by nature curious and avid for knowledge; to this I attributed man's honour, and I scorned the ignorant multitude. Rousseau set men right. He taught me to disregard a trifling privilege and to attribute to moral worth the true dignity of our species. Rousseau was in a certain sense the Newton of the moral order; he discovered in the realm of ethics that which makes for the unity of human nature, just as Newton found the principle which ties together all the laws of physical nature." He adds these sentences, which foreshadow in so remarkable a fashion his social conception of ethics: "Rousseau, moreover, had this idea, that wills can and should act one upon the other, that men should work for their mutual enlightenment. From this time on the *locus* of virtue no longer lies in individual perfection, but in the just relations of men to each other. *What is to be fashioned is a republic of wills.*"

Kant's view at that time was that our moral judgments are based upon a sentiment—the ethical sentiment—which he describes in his brief work, *Observations on the Sentiment of the Beautiful and the Sublime* (1764), as being particularly the *sentiment of the beauty and the dignity of human nature*. Yet even then he had some idea that sentiment as a foundation for ethics does not suffice, and in the same work he acknowledges that "true virtue can only be grafted on principles, and that the more universal are the latter, the more noble and elevated becomes the former." Here we come in contact with another characteristic which also will never leave Kant and which also will never leave Kant and which was to form a primary element in his system of morals: belief in the superiority of a directing ethical principal over all the other faculties of man. Soon (1770) the philosopher takes an altogether new position. Having worked out, by reason of his investigations into the nature of cognition which were to lead to the *Critique of Pure Reason*, a separation between experience and reason, between matter and form, and having assigned to reason and to form the power of conferring universality upon our process-of-knowing, he applies this distinction in the realm of ethics and from this comes to his celebrated thesis, wherein our moral concepts are based, not on experience, not on sentiment, but on pure reason. The reason itself supplies certain fixed judgments, which are neither deduced from anterior judgements, nor induced from experience, but are inherent in the nature of a "rational being." Here is the *formal* character of his ethics. Once again Kant has reached an essential point of his doctrine: the internal relation between action and law which, in his view, can exist only if the law is purely formal, that is to say, independent of experience. "Empirical principles," he says, "can never serve as bases for moral laws,"[12] a doctrine diametrically opposite to the classical ethics of happiness, according to which action is governed by considerations of interest (individual or collective), exclusively determined, or believing themselves so to be, by experience.

Kant's intellectual evolution, from the point of view with which we are here concerned and up to its final development in the *Critique of Practical Reason*, passes through a last phase of which the manifestations are, on the one hand, his *Anthropology*, his *Idea of a Universal History on a Cosmo-Political Plan* (1784) his *Conjectures on the Beginnings of the History of the Human Race* (1786) and, on the other hand, his *Fundamental Principles of the Metaphysic of Morals* (1785).

In the first group of books Kant, returning to the evolutionist considerations to which he had given his youthful adherence in his *Universal History of Nature*, decides upon a thoroughly pessimistic conception of human nature. He quotes with approval the answer of Frederick II to the optimist Sülzer: "My dear Sülzer, you have no idea what a damned breed we belonged to!" He is struck above all by the perverseness of men in their relations with each other. His consolation lies in hoping

---

12. *Fundamental Principles of the Metaphysic of Morals*, Second Section, Chapter III.

(wherefore he drew to himself, notably from Renouvier, the criticisms to which all evolutionists are subject) that the individual, through all his misdeeds and sufferings, would unconsciously but surely seek the good of the species, which is the practice of the rational life, and even that the intensification of the miseries of mankind (particularly of war) may perhaps be necessary to compel it eventually to that rational life. (One is reminded of the saying of Vauvenargues: "The passions have taught men reason.") This fulfilment would, moreover, only be possible through an association of free personalities, that is to say a cosmopolitical association (here Kant foretells a society of nations), though according to him if would be perhaps extremely hurtful if such a state of perfection were to be essayed prematurely. In *the Fundamental Principles of the Metaphysic of Morals* Kant points out that, given the judgments expressed by mankind on moral matters in social life, the question arises of finding out what principles determine them, and whether these principles, once they have been investigated, can be brought into unity. It was for this reason that Socrates took as subjects for his analyses common opinions on things (the δσξα) and sought to draw therefrom universal definitions. This method, Kant was to say, does not suffice. We know that in astronomy men were not satisfied with Kepler's laws, which had been drawn directly from observation, and that science had not been truly established until the day when Newton undertook to give an account of these empiric laws by deducing them from a principle drawn from the essential properties of matter. Accordingly to Kant the moralist should undertake a similar task. There we have a foreshadowing of the work in which our philosopher will give his ethics a definitive form, a work which we shall now discuss, the *Critique of Practical Reason* (1788).

In this work of capital importance, both for its author's intellectual evolution and for the place it occupies in the history of human thought, Kant assigns to ethics the goal of discovering and unravelling the principle which the reason of the practical man—the *practical reason*—uses without knowing it. He sets forth (1) ethical facts or data,) (2) the law which these facts attest, (3) the faculty which acts in accordance with this law.

According to Kant, the ordinary moral consciousness perceives quite clearly that the ethical value of an action does not depend upon its external results, but upon the interior will which gives it rise. Hence it follows that only that action is moral which springs from duty or respect for the moral law. Yielding to custom or to past experiences, however sublime, would not make an action moral. Morality therefore cannot derive from a subordination to authority, and thereby Kant separates ethics from a passive obedience to religious precepts. Already in the *Critique of Pure Reason* (*Transcendental Methodology*, II, 2) he had said that certain acts should be considered as divine commandments because inwardly binding, and not binding because they are considered as divine commandments. So also God, described as unknowable in this same work, cannot constitute a basis for ethics. Likewise ethics cannot proceed from sentiment, the latter being necessarily empirical, egoistic, and arising, in the last analysis, from an instinct for happiness, the opposite, according to Kant, of morality. The criterion of ethics is for Kant the *autonomy* or characteristic quality which the will has to be its own law. Kant opposes this quality to *heteronomy*, or the willingness to act in accordance with a motive foreign to the will, and which for him represents immorality. This interior law, implied in the practical reason, meets with opposition in us by virtue of our sensory, phenomenal, not exclusively rational, nature. That is why Kant calls it a *law*, which is expressed, he says, through an absolute injunction, a "categorical imperative." In this again he differs from the moralists of happiness, for whom the imperatives of ethics are always, in his own term, *hypothetical*; that is, subordinated to a definite end to be achieved. Finally—a necessary and not the least considerable consequence of this conception—duty requires that each one shall divest himself of all personal interest and all seeking after immediate happiness.

Now what is the content of this moral law? What task does it require of us? One only, answers Kant: that we respect the value of other persons, a value which lies in this, that they also are orientated toward autonomy. Kant's ethics therefore involves two essential commandments. The first, formulated in the *Fundamental Principles of the Metaphysic of Morals*, declares: "Act always as though the maxim of your action should be erected by your will into a universal law";[13] more precisely, according to an

---

13. Kant claims, among other things, that we should not lie. For if there were a universal right to tell lies, all the confidence men

especially authoritative interpreter of the master of Koenigsberg (Renouvier): "Act toward others in such fashion that if you supposed yourself in another's place, and he in yours, all other things being equal, the motive which caused you to act shall continue to seem as good to you as you found it good at the time of your action; your act will be moral only if it can measure up to this criterion." (A maxim which Kant holds is to be carefully distinguished from the "golden rule": "Do as you would be done by," which seems to him to have egoism as its basis.) The second commandment is this: "Act in such fashion that you always treat mankind, as much in your own person as in that of another, as an end, never as a means." But how can I treat others as an end without lowering myself to the rôle of a means? I can do so if all wills are in agreement and constitute what Kant calls a *kingdom of ends*. From whence this last formula: the foundation of all practical law-making lies in conceiving the will of each as universal, legislative will. For every one of us, morality lies

---

have in each other would by that very fact disappear. To me this seems a remarkable feature of Kant's teaching; vainly do I seek, among the philosophers who preceded Kant, in Descartes, in Spinoza, in Leibniz, a high regard for truth-telling, a condemnation of lying; I even find in Spinoza (*Theological-Political Treatise*, V 7) a certain praise of Machiavellianism. (Cf. No. 16: *The Living Thoughts of Machiavelli* presented by Count Carlo Sforza.) Here again, as I shall point out later, Kant seems to be a founder of social ethics. See a controversy on the right of lying between Kant and Benjamin Constant in the Introduction by A. Aulard, cited above.

in transferring his consciousness from individuality to universality.

Be it noted that, by virtue of the fact that for Kant the criterion of the moral act is its possibility of being erected into a moral law, his teaching differs radically from that of earlier moralists. These latter set up knowledge as a principal condition of morality, and thus made it, whether or not they so desired, the prerogative of the elect. Through its fundamental accessibility to all, Kantian ethics is homogeneous with Christianity.

Finally, obedience to the moral law, being in no sense a determined thing, but rather an effect of our will, implies the existence in us of a faculty to which Kant dedicated long study: freedom. According to him freedom belongs neither to the realm of experience, nor to the regions beyond experience, which are forbidden to our understanding. Freedom belongs to the reason, so much so that certain of those who came after him, seemingly faithful to his thought (the neo-Kantians), made of it a fundamental category of our mind, in the same order as space and time. All Kant's line of reasoning is summed up in this celebrated formula: "You can, because you should. (*Du kannst, denn du sollst.*)" This amounts to saying: the reason requires our obedience to the moral law; but that imperative would be meaningless if it were not possible for us either to conform or not to conform to that law. Hence it is enough to point out the necessary concurrence of the reason with itself to infer freedom from duty.

Again Kant defines as freedom whatever power we may

have to effect *absolute beginnings*. Under this aspect it is particularly easy to see that he excludes this faculty from the field of phenomena, since the latter, being governed by the principle of causality according to which everything that begins to exist has a cause, allow of only relative beginnings. And indeed, according to him, our freedom belongs to the *noumenal* order, in the order or *things-in-themselves*. Kant's idea is that each of us has a *double* of his person, which, inasmuch as it is noumenal, dwells outside experience, outside of time, and to the extent that it is such, is free; whereas one's phenomenal person submits to the illusions of causality. Moreover Kant attributes this duality of aspect to all phenomena; and it constitutes perhaps the most fundamental characteristic of his philosophy. For him the explanation of every phenomenon is dual: inasmuch as it appears in time, on the one hand, it is by necessity subject to connection with an anterior phenomenon, and is hence determined; inasmuch as it is a *thing-in-itself*, on the other hand, it has *causes outside of time, which are not phenomena*, and its connection with these causes constitutes its freedom, the latter being, therefore, a "transcendental" reality. As to Kant's preference for the one or the other of these two aspects, a preference, which, in very different fashion from his argumentation, indicates the depth of his nature, it bursts forth in this phrase, which he constantly repeats: "Phenomena in themselves are nothing." Indeed Kant's belief in liberty, like his belief in the existence of God, the immortality of the soul, comes to exist in him by means of faith, which he describes as "a moral state of the reason in the consent it gives to things inaccessible to the understanding." This definition implies these three premises of the will, to which one can hardly devote too much study, for they constitute the whole teaching of our philosopher on the subject we are considering: (1) faith is a *state of the reason*; (2) the reason can know a *moral* state; (3) it can consent to things inaccessible to the understanding. By declaring these objects of faith inaccessible to the understanding, Kant asserted that he detached himself from metaphysics, at least from the metaphysics he opposed, which laid claim to knowledge of those object.[14]

Such are, in brief review, the ethical ideas which engaged this great mind. It can be said that, without exception and in the most minute detail, they absorbed the attention of the most distinguished thinkers from Jacobi, Schopenhauer[15] and Hegel down to Boutroux, Höffding and Renouvier. It should be added that these ideas have given rise to serious criticisms on the part of these thinkers, side by side with the most hearty admiration.

---

14. Note here the injustice of that reproach so often made against Kant by the frivolous, that he fell back into metaphysics after he had so ably demonstrated its vanity. The metaphysics to which Kant opposed himself is that which undertakes to *appear as a science*. To that metaphysics Kant never consented. What he admitted was a strictly agnostic faith, another thing altogether, which his *Critique* in no way forbade him.
15. Cf. No. 1: *The Living Thoughts of Schopenhauer* presented by Thomas Mann.

Thus they have questioned whether Kant had not arbitrarily gone over from rationalism to an ethical rigorism in no wise included therein, and which was to be attributed to his personal preferences rather than to his logic; whether Kant, insetting up an ethical system, was justified in satisfying himself with enjoining us to retire into ourselves and to confine ourselves to our individual consciousness, or whether it would not have been better to observe all the manifestations of spiritual life, as they appear in history, sociology, psychology, and to try through analysis to extricate from them guiding principles; they have reproached him with having limited himself to a criticism of the common ethical notions which he had ready at hand rather than having established those notions on the basis of a comprehensive historical investigation. As for mankind in general, aware of general ideas but not especially versed in philosophic criticism, it has dropped from Kant's ethical system many a demonstration, many a classification, many a subsidiary synthesis, of which experts, as is their task, debate the validity. Mankind has retained from that system the following capital ideas, which I have for that reason marked with special emphasis in my recapitulation of the philosopher's evolution: the idea that ethics is something independent of theology and has a base of origin in the practical nature of man; the idea that our ethics can only be the outcome of our will, exercised in its autonomy, that is to say, freed of any reference to its objects; the idea of the independence of duty with regard to any system of ends based on interest, that is to say, a scorn for the ethics of utility or of happiness; finally the idea that the moral law extends beyond man's individual limits and requires that man shall look upon himself as a citizen in a kingdom of persons and consequently shall always consider the human person as an end, never as a means. These ideas have permeated the spiritual life of mankind, like some foreign substance in the life-blood of an individual, imparting to it a new complexion. They have become subjects for study, themes for literature (not to mention their being the object of violent hostility, as with Nietzsche or Barrès in his *The Uprooted*); they have created the concept of individual morality which does not necessarily involve membership in a Church; they have led to placing the emphasis in ethics on its social aspect rather than in considering it almost entirely as a set of duties toward oneself and toward God: they have indirectly influenced many statesmen, pushing them in the direction of political systems which tend toward greater respect for the person and greater civic solidarity, toward institutions which tend to extinguish national egoisms by means of a federative principle. To have given such movements their initial impetus, whatever may be their future, seems to me to assure Kant a place of honour and a place almost unparalleled in the ethical history of mankind.

I cannot bring to an end this discussion of Kant's ethical writings without some account of two books, published by him within the same year (1797), the *Philosophy of Law* and the *Principles of Virtue*. In spite of undeniable weaknesses arising from the advanced age of their author, they contain additional ideas which mankind

KANT 33

seems to have remembered. In the first of these writings Kant repeats his principle that a person should never be treated as a thing. This time he deduces from it not only individual freedom, but freedom of speech and the right of every citizen to participate in the making of laws. If follows that in his opinion the constitution of the future is republican (granting always that the republican spirit can be exercised in a monarchy) and that the State, whose "paternal" pretensions he repels and to which he refuses any capacity to make citizens happy in spite of themselves, has as its function to safeguard, not the happiness of its wards, but their liberty. In this one recognizes the Anglo-Saxon conception of government and one can see that it was not without reason that the apostle of such dogmas should, fifteen years earlier, have been filled with enthusiasm for the War of Independence of the North American colonies, even though he considered illegitimate, as a matter of right, recourse to force on the part of the people against their *de facto* sovereign, however good might be their cause. Perhaps he did not give enough consideration to the fact that, in denying force as a right with respect to subjects, he granted the right to force with respect to sovereigns.[16] In the *Principles of Virtue*, Kant,

---

16. Kant contrasts a republic to a democracy, which latter he considers a tyrannical form of government, quite obviously because he thinks he sees its fulfilment in the exceptional régime which France set up in 1793, when confronted with danger from abroad. He also opposes democracy through his repudiation of universal suffrage. (He refuses the right of suffrage to the poor because they are "dependent upon others"

without going so far as to accept the precept of positivism: *Live for others*, asserts that a useless and superfluous man in his person dishonours mankind. He considers it part of our duty to do good for the men, even though their true nature, according to him, scarcely incites us to love them. Perhaps he would be willing to attach high value, with his disciple Schopenhauer, to pity. In a curious chapter entitled "On Fawning," he refuses, like Spinoza, to consider humility a virtue, in that it is the denial of our dignity. It is likely that he would have informed Goethe, as did Beethoven in his famous reproach, that men of their quality had no business bowing and scraping before the great. It may by wondered whether he would not have said, again with the author of the *Ethics*, "Happiness is not the reward of virtue, but is virtue itself." Another theme developed in this book is that human love, instead of having value when considered purely as a feeling, as Tolstoi[17] was later to proclaim, has true moral greatness only if subject to the reason.

---

and because he grants it only to free citizens.)Yet if it be noted that he describes as republican any régime built upon "a system representative of the people, established to protect its rights in the people's name and by means of its delegates," a régime in which birth confers no privileges, where taxes, as a general rule, can be assessed only by virtue of the consent of the people's deputies, where the separation of governmental powers commands respect—one is led to believe that he would, in large measure, have approved of modern democracies.

17. Cf. No. 4: *The Living Thoughts of Tolstoi* presented by Stefan Zweig.

Then, finally, one of the achievements of Kant's ethical thought is his celebrated *Perpetual Peace*, natural complement to his *Philosophy of Law*. Far from proving himself therein a marker of Utopias, Kant asserts that such a good thing as eternal peace can only very slowly come to pass and that, given what humanity still is, even the best intentioned States would show wisdom in keeping their hands on the hilts of their swords. The coming of a definitive peace among men seems to him to be bespoken by their own deepest nature, but thwarted principally by men of state. Of these, some sincerely desire this consummation, but work for it as though it were a problem of *political technique*, whereas it is in the moral order and requires on the part of peoples adherence to *formal* principles which are independent of *material considerations*. Others, in the bottom of their hearts pushing aside the prospect of such a future, apply themselves, by means of more or less sophistical maxims concerning "the impossibility of making mankind better" or by asserting the right of certain nations to oppress all others, to maintain among their subjects the cult of war, from which they expect to profit. (Today Kant could add to these, certain "moralists," the existence of whom he said he could not conceive, who set about—Nietzsche, for example—playing the game of those politicians who are devoted to the perpetuation of war and who commit what a present-day writer has called *The Treason of the Intellectuals*.)[18] His hop is the setting up, not of a super-

---

18. Julien Benda: *The Treason of the Intellectuals*.

State which would insure peace through its domination over others, but of an association of states in which each would preserve its individuality and its liberty; the setting up of what he calls *cosmo-political law*, namely, one "in which men or States are considered as exerting influence the one on the other by reason of their being constituent parts of the great State of the human race." If I add that his maxims express ideas like this one: "In a war one should not allow oneself to commit acts of warfare of such a kind as to make reciprocal confidence impossible when it comes time to make peace"; or again, "Since a violation of rights in one part of the earth is felt in *all* parts, the setting up of a civil law for the world becomes a necessity for States and for peoples"; or again, "It is true of peoples, considered as States, just as it is of individuals, that if they live in a state of nature and without laws, their neighbourship alone acts as an injury," such ideas, I think, make it easy enough to see how dramatically modern is this little treatise.

IV

Kant's ideas on religion, or, more precisely, on the relation between his conception of the world and his ethical doctrine, he expressed in the *Critique of Pure Reason*, in the *Critique of Practical Reason*, and above all in his book entitled *Religion within the Limits of Reason Alone* (1793). They are seemingly a result of his pietistic education and show us the embodiment of a will, rather than depending—however much they may claim to do so—upon rigorous argumentation. Hence it follows that they especially have given the logicians occasion to exercise their rigour.

Thus Kant *desires* that anyone who is truly imbued with the moral law should by that very fact be induced to believe in the existence of God and in the immortality of the person, these "religious postulates" being, in his view, the necessary conditions for the fulfilment of that law. He desires (as we have seen he did for freedom) that the practical reason entail consequences relating to something situated outside the boundaries established by the reason, that that something (the thing-in-itself), essentially unknowable by the reason, should become conceivable to us, if not knowable, by virtue of our giving effect to the need aroused in us by the *practical* reason for postulating a total realization of all our moral ideals. (He calls this, where belief in the existence of God is concerned, a *cosmic* use of our reason.) Yet he insists upon these postulates when at the same time, in Pure Reason, he asserts that there cannot be any duty which would force us to believe that which is unknowable, and when religious psychology—*religious experience*, as it later came to be called—could already have shown him instances where the sense of duty in no way entails beliefs of this sort and where man, although devoid of religion, is still unquestionably moral. So likewise it has seemed astonishing to find him maintaining that, in the absence of such postulates, a man could not strive after the *end* which the moral law proposes; when at the same time he forbade, in the practice of that law, all thought of ends and wished that it should find satisfaction in itself, without troubling itself over the results which it might produce. Others have pointed to the difficulty which lies in his adopting a real doctrine of a divine person, which is basically irreconcilable with the philosophy of the infinite that flows through all his thought. So also is it with the arbitrary way in which he sets up the idea of a Supreme Being while requiring us to remain completely indifferent to the matter of knowing whether this idea be true or false, an enquiry of such nature being according to him contrary to reason, while at the same time he enjoins us to make this idea a principle for action with regard to our individual and social conduct.

However well founded such criticisms may be, still, from the point of view of the historian of man as a moral being, to Kant belongs the honour of having restored in a particularly profound way the religious problem to a personal need, determined by the relations between the person and his ethical ideals, rather than letting it consist in passive submission to an external authority and in the mechanical performance of ritual acts. Kant also seems to deserve the gratitude of all those concerned with the spiritual progress of mankind when he insists that the God Who is within us is alone qualified to evaluate anything which offers itself for consideration by virtue of claiming to be revealed truth, "moral law," says he, "being safer than any faith"; as well as when he insists that the kingdom of God is consequently not a kingdom of priests, on whom historical erudition and an ability to read the Scriptures confer a monopoly of union with the Divine, but is a world open to all those who, through the sincerity of their hearts, discover themselves to have immediate and intimate intercourse with truth. He expresses this in another way by hoping that the temporal Church may little by little give up its authoritarian character and may come closer and closer to being a true Church. As one reads these passages, on thinks of Chateaubriand and Ernest Renan, declaring that Christianity, far from being definitely formulated, is in process of formation, and that it is the future which will witness its true fulfilment. Here again Kant seems to have set in motion important spiritual movements which the ages that followed him were to develop, and seems to justify the saying of Goethe, that the mark of a genius is the power to stimulate activity after his death.

V

In his last great work, the *Critique of Judgment* (1790), Kant, at the age of sixty-seven, seems to me to have achieved one of the most exalted and most genuine, because most noble, of his ideas, even if it did not have the most effect upon mankind. He was always preoccupied with the desire to find a principle of universality in the emotions of man; he believed he had found it pre-eminently in the feeling for the beautiful, this feeling in his opinion being fixed in something which is common to all men—the need for a harmonious relation between the faculty of intuition and the faculty of understanding. (In contrast to the views of recent schools of thought, the faculty of understanding constituted for Kant a basic element in the aesthetic sentiment.) This sentiment (or feeling), by reason of its character of universality (as well as its disinterestedness) would then in very profound fashion be related to the ethical sentiment. A corollary of this notion, which was to be developed by Schopenhauer, is that music is a particularly moral art; and one cannot help thinking of Richard Wagner who, as a disciple of Kant through the agency of the author of the *World as Will and Idea*, asserted that by establishing the Bayreuth theatre and by inviting thousands of men from every country to come there for artistic communion, he worked more effectively for peace than many an officially pacifist institution.

Proceeding then to the question of artistic creation, Kant sees therein a particularly complete exercise of freedom and of the emancipation of the human person from external needs; thereby opens up the important idea, later developed with so much brilliance (by Schiller in his *Letters on the Aesthetic Education of Man*, by Guyau in his *Art from the Sociological Point of View*), of the moral value inherent in artistic activity. Here is an appropriate moment to point out what one might call the point of co-ordination of Kant's work, that is the point where all the values, apparently disparate, which he extols become related. This point is the threefold quality of universality, freedom and disinterestedness.

In the second part of his *Critique of Judgment*, the part which deals with biological considerations and is called Teleological Judgment, Kant can claim the glory of having been the first to furnish principles for those thinkers who, from the beginning of the nineteenth century on, would seek to rise above the mere recording of facts and formulate philosophical ideas about the biological order. Postulating finality as a natural law inseparable from organization, holding as *an end of nature* that *process* which is "an organized being organizing itself"[19] (here we find again his religion of the will), he therefore admits in the phenomena of life a causality different from mechanism; in other words he sees in the organizing activity of nature a cause altogether different from those of which we have knowledge. Moreover these assertions are made by Kant as necessities of our reason,[20] not as the results of observation (we think of organisms, *as if* they were effects of a directing intelligence). These assertions in no way prevent the thinker from considering it his duty to account for biological phenomena as much as possible by mechanism, for example to hope for "some new Newton who would one day come to account for the production

---

19. Kant here makes a distinction, since become classic, between *internal* finality, in accordance with which every organism would have *in itself* the conditions sufficient and necessary for life, and *external* finality, or adaptation of that organism to its environment. Modern philosophy is inclined not to admit any finality as internal. Cf. D. Roustan, *Leçons de Philosophie*, Volume I, Chapter XIII, "The Principle of Finality."
20. Here Kant could call for a *teleological* state of the reason, as he conceived a *cosmic* state of the reason in connection with belief in a Supreme Being, and, for a consent to the imperatives of ethics, a *moral* state of the same faculty. The originality of his teachings, and their unity, lies in all these attitudes being for him states *of the reason*.

of a blade of grass by natural laws over which no 'design' has had authority." Then again the common origin which one can attribute to different forms of life by reason of their basic analogy, as well as the idea that nature could gradually have developed, by consequence of a previous design, from rudimentary living forms to others better suited to their environment, he represents as being only hypotheses, attractive but dangerous suggestions of the reason. Here he differs radically from such modern philosophers as, expressing views on "creative" evolution even less subject to proof (that evolution, for instance, works through the ages in accordance with the same law as governs the consciousness of the individual), express these views as interpretations of scientific experience. As to the antagonism between the formation of an organism by a blind assembling of its parts and its formation by an ordered synthesis, it could well, say Kant, be due merely to the nature of our reason, mechanism and finality then depending upon a single principle, but a principle for which our reason is incapable of supplying a formula. In this we find once more Kant's basic idea, which supplies an underlying theme for the *Critique of Pure Reason*, namely that that which arouses in us the concept of causality is basically the same as that which establishes the order the world; in other words that there is connection between the law of our mind and those of reality. In this Kant's opposite is Spinoza, who insists that we see order in the world only because we attribute imagination to God; not that God, being the essence of the world, know nothing of the intelligence, but that the intelligence which is proper to him differs from the animal of the same name. Here is a scorn for the human race, in the name of pantheism, necessarily and totally unknown to that philosopher for whom morality is the supreme virtue.

In this same last part of his book Kant repeats, and states more precisely, his affirmation, previously made in *Idea of a Universal History*, that nature, despite the atrocious behaviour she presently forces upon us (individuals as well as states) and will do for a long period of history, has as final end the morality of the species. Specifically, nature admits of a moral end: *culture* (that is to say the exercise of freedom on behalf of the moral law); and teaches us discipline. It has been easy enough to object against him that culture, as he understands it, and discipline, far from being products of nature, are eminently victories over nature, and easy enough to point out the contradiction between his optimism with regard to the ends he attributes to nature and the pessimism, so pronounced in him, with regard to the means used by that same nature to achieve her ends. Perhaps it would be fairer not to scrutinize so closely the logical coherence of this work, but rather to remember its intent, which is manifest in such a passage as this: "Through the nature of things, I understand human nature. Because a respect for right and for duty ever dwells therein, I cannot and would not believe it so submerged in evil that the normally practical reason should not end by triumphing over it and making it altogether worthy of love." It is scarcely necessary to ask whether every man, by virtue of his humanity, will not at once perceive the nobility of such a sentiment.

VI

If, in conclusion, we now take the point of view which the publisher of this series would have us take in judging the work of a philosopher, if we ask what is still living, that is effectively living, in the work of Kant, our answer would be that almost the whole of that work remains such, but in two very different ways. The basic theses of the *Critique of Pure Reason* and the *Critique of Judgment* are still eminently living in the sense that, explicitly or not, they are a vital element in all modern philosophic writing which relates either to the study of cognition or to speculation in aesthetics or biology. Still it can be said that they have lost something of their vitality in the sense that, after having aroused at the time of, and long after, their appearance violent resistance, they have today, as it were, fallen into the public domain, and have been assimilated into the thinking of mankind as banal truths which no longer cause discussion. Indeed it no longer occurs to any serious thinker to question the existence of forms of the mind which are independent of experience, or which at least have become so with the passage of time, or to question the special quality of freedom and disinterestedness attaching to the aesthetic sentiment, or the necessity of appealing to some finality in order to account for vital phenomena in any philosophic spirit. In like manner no one struggles to deny that the thing-in-itself, if it exists at all, belongs to the unknowable and that certain questions put to us by the pageant of life relate to faith and not to knowledge.

KANT 45

The same does not at all hold true for the ethical portion of Kant's work; and, on the contrary, it can well be said that here his theses, which fifty years ago seemed definitely accepted by mankind, and for that very reason deprived of vital quality inasmuch as life implies activity, are the object of an opposition which is organized and more resolute than ever before and that from this point of view they have acquired a tremendous renewal of vitality. And indeed, whereas fifty years ago the main ideas of the Kantian ethic ran up against only a few isolated adversaries, regarded by almost all serious-mined men as eccentrics, today they are opposed by teachers with followings mentors who solemnly preach the moral value of an unbridled use of "life"—"dynamism"—and cannot show enough scorn for any moderating conception of duty;[21] whose only ethics consists in yielding to "facts" in their "fatality"—biology and history (which they order in accordance with their own needs)—and who overwhelm with their sarcasm those who would redress man's injustice by means of man's will; who loudly assert that man's true nobility lies in war, that those who would settle their differences by pacific means are either hypocrites or

---

21. Kant always excoriated the religion of "life." In 1782, in a poem which he composed upon the death of Pastor Lilienthal, who had married Kant's parents, he wrote:
    Was auf das Leben folgt deckt tiefe Finsterniss;
    Was uns zu thun gebührt, dess sind wir nur gewiss.
    (What comes after life is hidden in deep darkness;
    What we are expected to do, that alone we know.)

cowards. Today the Kantian ethic meets up with established schools of thought, which openly teach youth, whose attention they tirelessly seek to enlist, that the only morality worth prizing is the "master morality," which is practised "beyond good and evil," with all its inevitable cruelties; that the doctrine of the rights of man and the equality of citizens before the law constitutes the shame of mankind. And the Kantian ethic meets up with great States which officially proclaim that ethics consists, for the individual, in silencing the precepts of his personal conscience, the Kantian "autonomy," and obeying only those of the State; and consists, for the State, in considering the citizen not as a person but as a thing,[22] whilst its duty as a State is to ridicule the pretensions of universal morality with its fixed principles, claiming to be superior to individual interests,[23] and to seek only the immediate advantage of its population, with whatever may be involved therein by way of violation of contractual obligations and of scorn for the rights of others—to recognize only relative truths, established by the needs of its social organism and changing with those needs. It is against this ethics, become so powerful that it has seemed on the point of possessing the world, it is against this ethics of "pragmatism" or the sovereignty of

---

22. "The function of a true State is so to act that individuals do not exist." Hegel, *Philosophy of the Mind*, II, 7.
23. "The essence of an inferior people is to believe in something immutable." Fichte, *Seventh Discourse to the German People*.

the end,[24] that other States have finally risen up. If the thought of a philosopher lives to the extent that it arouses in the present generation a will to defend it, with a full acceptance of the sacrifices involved in such a decision, the philosopher who sleeps under the shadows of Koenigsberg can assure himself that his thought, even though our young soldiers rarely mention his name, is more living than ever. Need I add with what passionate concern those for whom the worth of the world rests upon respect for human dignity and freedom follow their battle and invoke their victory, as he also very probably would have done himself.

---

24. Need I remind the reader that this ethics is also that of Marxism? We know that one of the main principles of this philosophy is to denounce the fondness of some men or those precepts of conscience styled "transcendental," to that which Marx pityingly calls the "divine" part in mankind, and to assert that the human race will continue enslaved so long as it does not free itself of these miserable notions. So also this system allows of no fixed truth, but only of a truth entirely based upon the needs of the moment. In Stalin's *Report on the Five Year Plan* can be read a moving apologia for the principle of contradiction, considered as a "value of life" and "an instrument of struggle." As to the will to treat the human person as a thing, the action of the Soviet government toward a certain neighbouring small country, and action of which the Soviet is proud, shows well enough that this will, for the followers of Marx, is one of the noble values.

Critique of Pure Reason

Preface

Whether the treatment of that class of knowledge with which reason is occupied follows the secure method of a science or not, can easily be determined by the result. If, after repeated preparations, it comes to a standstill, as soon as its real goal is approached, or is obliged, in order to reach it, to retrace its steps again and again, and strike into fresh paths; again, if it is impossible to produce unanimity among those who are engaged in the same work, as to the manner in which their common object should be obtained, we may be convinced that such a study is far from having attained to the secure method of a science, but is groping only in the dark. In that case we are conferring a great benefit on reason, if we only find out the right method, though many things should have to be surrendered as useless, which were comprehended in the original aim that had been chosen without sufficient reflection.

That *Logic*, from the earliest times, has followed that secure method, may be seen from the fact that since *Aristotle* it has not had to retrace a single step, unless we choose to consider as improvements the removal of some unnecessary subtleties or the clearer definition of its matter, both of which refer to the elegance rather than to the solidity of the science. It is remarkable also, that to that present day, it has not been able to make one step in advance, so that, to all appearance, it may be considered as completed and perfect. If some modern philosophers thought to enlarge it, by introducing *psychological* chapters on the different faculties of knowledge (faculty of imagination, wit, etc.), or *metaphysical* chapters on the origin of knowledge, or the different degrees of certainty according to the different objects (idealism, scepticism, etc.), or lastly, *anthropological* chapters on prejudices, their causes and remedies, this could only arise from their ignorance of the peculiar nature of logical science. We do not enlarge, but we only disfigure the sciences, *if we allow* their respective limits to be confounded: and the limits of logic are definitely fixed by the fact, that it is a science which has nothing to do but fully to exhibit and strictly to prove all formal rules of thought (whether it be *a priori* or empirical, whatever be its origin or its object, and whatever be the impediments, accidental or natural, which it has to encounter in the human mind).

That logic should in this respect have been so successful, is due entirely to its limitation, whereby it has not only the right, but the duty, to make abstraction of all the objects of knowledge and their differences, so that that understanding has to deal with nothing beyond itself and its own forms. It was, of course, far more difficult for reason to enter on the secure method of science, when it has to deal not with itself only, but also with objects. Logic, therefore, as a kind of preparation (*propaedeutic*) forms, as it were, the vestibule of the sciences only, and where real knowledge is concerned, is presupposed for critical purposes only, while the acquisition of knowledge must be sought for in the sciences themselves, properly and objectively so called.

If there is to be in those sciences an element of reason, something in them must be known a priori, and knowledge may stand in a twofold relation to its object, by either simply *determining* it and its concept (which must be supplied from elsewhere), or by making it *real* also. The former is *theoretical*, the latter *practical knowledge* of reason. In both the *pure* part, namely, that in which reason determines its object entirely *a priori* (whether it contain much or little), must be treated first, without mixing up with it what comes from other sources; for it is bad economy to spend blindly whatever comes in, and not to be able to determine, when there is a stoppage, which part of the income can bear the expenditure, and where reductions must be made.

Mathematics and *physics* are the two theoretical sciences of reason, which have to determine their *objects a priori*; the former quite purely, the latter partially so, and partially from other sources of knowledge besides reason.

Mathematics, from the earliest times to which the history of human reason can reach, has followed, among that wonderful people of the Greeks, the safe way of a science. But it must not be supposed that it was as easy for mathematics as for logic, in which reason is concerned with itself alone, to find, or rather to make for itself that royal road. I believe, on the contrary that there was a long period of tentative work (chiefly still among the Egyptians) and that the change is to be ascribed to a *revolution*, produced by the happy thought of a single man, whose experiment pointed unmistakably to the path that had to be followed, and opened and traced out for the most distant times the safe way of a science. The history of that intellectual revolution, which was far more important than the discovery of the passage round the celebrated Cape of Good Hope, and the name of its fortunate author, have not been preserved for us. But the story preserved by Diogenes Laertius, who names the reputed author of the smallest elements of ordinary geometrical demonstration, even of such as, according to general opinion, do not require to be proved, shows, at all events, that the memory of the revolution, produced by the very first traces of the discovery of a new method, appeared extremely important to the mathematicians, and thus remained unforgotten. A new light flashed on the first man who demonstrated the properties of the isosceles triangle (whether his name was *Thales* or any other name), for he found that he had not to investigate what he saw in the figure, or the mere concept of that figure, and thus to learn its properties; but that he had to produce (by construction) what he had himself, according to concepts *a priori*, placed into that figure and represented in it, so that, in order to know anything with certainty *a priori*, he must not attribute to that figure anything beyond what necessarily follows from what he has himself placed into it, in accordance with the concept.

It took a much longer time before physics entered on the high way of science: for no more than a century and a half has elapsed since Bacon's ingenious proposal partly initiated that discovery, partly, as others were already on the right track, gave a new impetus to it—a discovery which, like the former, can only be explained by a rapid intellectual revolution. In what I have to say, I shall confine myself to natural science, so far as it is founded on *empirical* principles.

When Galilei let balls of a particular weight, which he had determined himself, roll down an inclined plane; or Torricelli made the air carry a weight, which he had previously determined to be equal to that of a definite volume of water; or when, in later times, Stahl[1] changed metal into lime, and lime again into metals, by withdrawing and restoring something, a new light flashed on all students of nature. They comprehended that reason has insight into that only, which she herself produces on her own plan, and that she must move forward with the principles of her judgments, according to fixed law, and compel nature to answer her questions, but not let herself be led by nature, as it were in leading strings, because

---

1. I am not closely following here the course of the history of the experimental method, nor are the first beginnings of it very well-known.

otherwise accidental observations, made on no previously fixed plan, will never converge towards a necessary law, which is the only thing that reason seeks and requires. Reason, holding in one hand its principles, according to which concordant phenomena alone can be admitted as laws of nature, and in the other hand the experiment, which it has devised according to those principles, must approach nature, in order to be taught by it: but not in the character of a pupil, who agrees to everything the master likes, but as an appointed judge, who compels the witnesses to answer the questions which he himself proposes. Therefore even the science of physics entirely owes the beneficial revolution in its character to the happy thought, that we ought to seek in nature (and not import into it by means of fiction) whatever reason must learn from nature, and could not know by itself, and that we must do this in accordance with what reason itself has originally placed into nature. Thus only has the study of nature entered on the secure method of a science, after having for many centuries done nothing but grope in the dark.

Metaphysics, a completely isolated and speculative science of reason, which declines all teaching of experience, and rests on concepts only (not on their application to intuition, as mathematics), in which reason therefore is meant to be her own pupil, has hitherto not been so fortunate as to enter on the secure path of a science, although it is older than all other science, and would remain, even if all the rest were swallowed up in the abyss of an all-destroying barbarism. In metaphysic, reason, even if it tries only to understand a *priori* (as it pretends to do) those laws which are confirmed by the commonest experience, is constantly brought to a standstill, and we are obliged again and again to retrace our steps, because they do not lead us where we want to go; while as to any unanimity among those who are engaged in the same work, there is so little of it in metaphysic, that it has rather become an arena, specially destined, it would seem, for those who wish to exercise themselves in mock fights, and where no combatant has, as yet, succeeded in gaining an inch of ground that he could call permanently his own. It cannot be denied, therefore, that the method of metaphysic has hitherto consisted in groping only, and, what is the worst, in groping among mere concepts.

What then can be the cause that hitherto no secure method of science has been discovered? Shall we say that it is impossible? Then why should nature have visited our reason with restless aspiration to look for it, as if it were its most important concern? Nay more, how little should we be justified in trusting our reason if, with regard to one of the most important objects we wish to know, it not only abandons us, but lures us on by vain hopes, and in the end betrays us! Or, if hitherto we have only failed to meet with the right path, what indications are there to make us hope that, if we renew our researches, we shall be more successful than others before us?

The examples of mathematics and natural science, which by one revolution have become what they now are, seem to me sufficiently remarkable to induce us to consider, what may have been the essential element in that intellectual revolution which has proved so beneficial to them, and to make the experiment, at least, so far as the analogy between them, as sciences of reason, with metaphysic allows it, of imitating them. Hitherto it has been supposed that all our knowledge must conform to the objects: but, under that supposition, all attempts to establish anything about them *a priori*, by means of concepts, and thus to enlarge our knowledge, have come to nothing. The experiment therefore ought to be made, whether we should not succeed better with the problems of metaphysic, by assuming that the objects must conform to our mode of cognition, for this would better agree with the demanded possibility of an *a priori* knowledge of them, which is to settle something about objects, before they are given to us. We have here the same case as with the first thought of Copernicus, who not being able to get on in the explanation of the movements of the heavenly bodies, as long as he assumed that all the stars turned round the spectator, tried, whether he could not succeed better, by assuming the spectator to be turning round, and the stars to be at rest. A similar experiment may be tried in metaphysic, so far as the *intuition* of objects is concerned. If the intuition had to conform to the constitution of objects, I do not see how we could know anything of it *a priori*; but if the objects (as an object of the senses) conforms to the constitution of our faculty of intuition, I can very well conceive such a possibility. As, however, I cannot rest in these intuitions, if they are to become knowledge, but have to refer them, as representations, to something as their object, and must determine that object by them, I have the choice of admitting, either that the *concepts*, by which I carry that determination, conform to the object, being then again in the same perplexity on account of the manner how I can know anything about it *a priori*; or that the objects, or what is the same, the experience in which alone they are known (as given objects), must conform to those concepts. In the latter case, the solution becomes more easy, because experience, as a kind of knowledge, requires understanding, and I must therefore, even before objects are given to me, presuppose the rules of the understanding as existing within me *a priori*, these rules being expressed in concepts *a priori*, to which all objects experience must necessarily conform, and with which they must agree. With regard to object, so far as they are conceived by reason only, and conceived as necessary, and which can never be given in experience, at least in that form in which they are conceived by reason, we shall find that the attempts at conceiving them (for they must admit of being conceived) will furnish afterwards an excellent test of our new method of thought, according to which we do not know of things anything a *priori* except what we ourselves put into them.[2]

---

2. This method, borrowed from the student of nature, consists in our looking for the elements of pure reason in that *which can be confirmed or refuted by experiment*. Now it is impossible, in order to test the propositions of pure reason, particularly if they venture beyond all the limits of possible experience, to make any experiment with their *objects* (as in natural science); we can therefore only try with *concepts* and *propositions* which we

This experiment succeeds as well as we could desire, and promises to metaphysic, in its first part, which deals with concepts *a priori*, of which the corresponding objects may be given in experience, the secure method of a science. For by thus changing our point of view, the possibility of knowledge *a priori* can well be explained, and, what is still more, the laws which *a priori* lie at the foundation of nature, as the sum total of the objects of experience, may be supplied with satisfactory proofs, neither of which was possible with the procedure hitherto adopted. But there arises from this deduction of our faculty of knowing *a priori*, as given in the first part of metaphysic, a somewhat startling result, apparently most detrimental to the object of metaphysic that have to be treated in the second part, namely, the impossibility of going with it beyond the frontier of possible experience, which is precisely the most essential purpose of metaphysical science. But here we have exactly the experiment which by disproving the opposite, establishes the truth of our first estimate of the knowledge of reason *a priori*, namely, that

---

admit *a priori*, by so contriving that the same object may be considered on one side as objects of the senses and of the understanding in experience, and, on the *other*, as objects which are only thought, intended, it may be, for the isolated reason which strives to go beyond all the limits of experience. This gives us two different sides to be looked at; and if we find that, by looking on things from that twofold point of view, there is an agreement with the principle of pure reason, while by admitting one point of view only, there arises an inevitable conflict with reason, then the experiment decides in favour of the correctness of that distinction.

it can refer to phenomena only, but must leave the thing by itself as unknown to us, though as existing by itself. For that which impels us by necessity to go beyond the limits of experience and of all phenomena, is the *unconditioned*, which reason postulates in all things by themselves, by necessity and by right, for everything conditioned, so that the series of conditions should thus become complete. If then we find that, under the supposition of our experience conforming to the objects as things by themselves, it is *impossible to conceive* the unconditioned *without contradiction*, while, under the supposition of our representation of things, as they are given to us, not conforming to them as things by themselves, but, on the contrary, of the objects conforming to our mode of representation, that *contradiction vanishes*, and that therefore the unconditioned must not be looked for in things, so far as we know them (so far as they are given to us), but only so far as we do not know them (as things by themselves), we clearly perceive that, we at first assumed tentatively only is fully confirmed.[3] But, after all

---

3. This experiment of pure reason has a great similarity with that of the *chemists*, which they sometimes call the experiment of *reduction*, or the *synthetical process* in general. The *analysis* of the *metaphysician* divided pure knowledge *a priori* into two very heterogeneous elements, namely, the knowledge of things as phenomena and of things by themselves. *Dialectic* combines these two again, to bring them into harmony with the necessary idea of the *unconditioned*, demanded by reason, and then finds that this harmony can never be obtained, except through the above distinction, which therefore must be supposed to be true.

progress in the field of the supersensuous has thus been denied to speculative reason, it is still open to us to see, whether in the practical knowledge of reason *data* may not be found which enable us to determine the transcendent concept of the unconditioned which is demanded by reason, in order thus, according to the wish of metaphysic, to get beyond the limits of all possible experience, by means of our knowledge *a priori*, which is possible to us for practical purposes only. In this case, speculative reason has at least gained for us room for such an extension of knowledge, though it had to leave it empty, so that we are not only at liberty, but are really called upon to fill it up, if we are able, by *practical data* of reason.[4]

The very object of the critique of pure speculative reason consists in this attempt at changing the old

---

4. In the same manner the laws of gravity, determining the movements of the heavenly bodies, imparted the character of established certainty to what Copernicus had assumed at first as an hypothesis only, and proved at the same time the invisible force (the Newtonian attraction) which holds the universe together, which would have remained for ever undiscovered, if Copernicus had not dared, by an hypothesis, which, though contradicting the senses, was yet true, to seek the observed movements, not in the heavenly bodies, but in the spectator. I also propose in this preface my own view of metaphysic, which has so many analogies with the Copernican hypothesis, as an hypothesis only, though in the Critique itself, it is proved by means of our representations of space and time, and the elementary concepts of the understanding, not hypothetically, but apodictically; for I wish that people should observe the first attempts at such a change, which must always be hypothetical.

procedure of metaphysic, and imparting to it the secure method of a science, after having completely revolutionized it, following the example of geometry and physical science. That critique is a treatize on the method (*Traité de la méthode*), not a system of the science itself; but it marks out nevertheless the whole plan of that science, both with regard to its limits, and to its internal organization. For pure speculative reason has this peculiar advantage that it is able, nay, bound to measure its own powers, according to the different ways in which it chooses its own object, and to completely enumerate the different ways of choosing problems: thus tracing a complete outline of a system of metaphysic. This is due to the fact that, with regard to the first point, nothing can be attributed to objects in knowledge *a priori*, except what the thinking subject takes from within itself; while, with regard to the second point, reason, so far as its principles of cognition are concerned, forms a separate and independent unity, in which, as in an organic body, every member exists for the sake of all others, and all others exist for the sake of the one, so that no principle can be safely applied in *one* relation, unless it has been carefully examined in *all* its relations, to the whole employment of pure reason. Hence, too, metaphysic has this singular advantage, an advantage which cannot be shared by any other science, in which reason has to deal with objects (for *Logic* deals only with the form of thought in general) that, if it has once attained, by means of this critique, to the secure method of a science, it can completely comprehend the whole field of knowledge pertaining to it, and thus finish its work and leave it to posterity, as a capital that can never be added to, because it has only to deal with principles and the limits of their employment, which are fixed by those principles themselves. And this completeness becomes indeed an obligation, if it is to be a fundamental science, of which we must be able to say *"nil actum reputans, si quid superesset agendum."*

But it will be asked, what kind of treasure is it which we mean to bequeath to posterity in this metaphysic of ours, after it has been purified by criticism, and thereby brought to a permanent condition? After a superficial view of this work, it may seem that its advantage is *negative* only, warning us against venturing with speculative reason beyond the limits of experience. Such is no doubt its primary use: but it becomes positive, when we perceive that the principles with which speculative reason ventures beyond its limits; lead inevitably, not to an *extension*, but, if carefully considered, to *narrowing* of the employment of reason, because, by indefinitely extending the limits of sensibility, to which they properly belong, they threaten entirely to supplant the pure (practical) employment of reason. Hence our *critique*, by limiting sensibility to its proper sphere, is no doubt *negative*; but by thus removing an impediment, which threatened to narrow, or even entirely to destroy its practical employment, it is in reality of *positive*, and of very important use, if only we are convinced that there is an absolutely necessary practical use of pure reason (the moral use), in which reason must inevitably go beyond the limits of sensibility, and though not requiring for this purpose the assistance of speculative reason, must at all events be assured against its opposition, lest it be brought in conflict with itself. To deny that this service, which is rendered by criticism, is a *positive* advantage, would be the same as to deny that the police confers upon us any positive advantage, its principal occupation being to prevent violence, which citizen have to apprehend from citizens, so that each may pursue his vocation in peace and security. We had established in the analytical part of our critique the following points: First, that space and time are only forms of sensuous intuition, therefore conditions of the existence of things, as phenomena only; Secondly, that we have no concepts of the understanding, and therefore nothing whereby we can arrive at the knowledge of things, except in so far as an intuition corresponding to these concepts can be given, and consequently that we cannot have knowledge of any object, as a thing by itself, but only in so far as it is an object of sensuous intuition, that is, a phenomenon. This proves no doubt that all speculative knowledge of reason is limited to objects of *experience*; but it should be carefully borne in mind, that this leaves it perfectly open to us, to *think* the same objects as things by themselves, though we cannot know them.[5] For otherwise we should

---

5. In order to *know* an object, I must be able to prove its possibility, either from its reality, as attested by experience, or *a priori* by means of reason. But I can *think* whatever I please, provided only I do not contradict myself, that is, provided my conception is a possible thought, though I may be unable to answer for the existence of a corresponding object in the sum total of all possibilities. Before I can attribute to such a concept objective

arrive at the absurd conclusion, that there is phenomenal appearance without something that appears. Let us suppose that the necessary distinction, established in our critique, between things as objects of experience and same things by themselves, had not been made. In that case, the principle of causality, and with it the mechanism of nature, as determined by it, would apply to all things in general, as efficient causes. I should then not be able to say of one and the same thing, for instance the human soul, that its will is free, and, at the same time, subject to the necessity of nature, that is, not free, without involving myself in a palpable contradiction: and this because I had taken the soul, in both propositions, in *one and the same sense*, namely, as a thing in general (as something by itself), as, without previous criticism, I could not but take it. If, however, our criticism was true, in teaching us to take an object in two senses, namely, either as a phenomenon, or as a thing by itself, and if the deduction of our concepts of the understanding was correct, and the principle of causality applies to things only, if taken in the first sense, namely, so far as they are objects of experience, but not to things, if taken in their second sense, we can, without any contradiction, think the same will when phenomenal (in visible actions) as necessarily conforming to the law of

---

reality (real possibilities, as distinguished from the former, which is purely logical), something more is required. This something more, however, need not be sought for in the sources of theoretical knowledge, for it may be found in those of practical knowledge also.

nature, and so far, *not free*, and yet, on the other hand, when belonging to a thing by it self, as not subject to that law of nature, and therefore *free*. Now it is quite true that I may not *know* my soul, as a thing by itself, by means of speculative reason (still less through empirical observation), and consequently may not know freedom either, as the quality of a being as determined in its existence, and yet as not determined in time (which, as I cannot provide my concept with any intuition, is impossible). This, however, does not prevent me from *thinking* freedom; that is, my representation of it contains of the two modes of representation (the sensible and the intelligible), and the consequent limitation of the concepts of the pure understanding, and of the principles based on them, has been properly carried out. If, then, morality necessarily presupposed freedom (in the strictest sense) as a property of our will, producing, as *a priori data* of it, practical principles, belonging originally to our reason, which, without freedom, would be absolutely impossible, while speculative reason had proved that such a freedom cannot even be thought, the former supposition, namely, the moral one, would necessarily have to yield to another, the opposite of which involves a palpable contradiction, so that *freedom*, and with it morality (for its opposite contains no contradiction, unless freedom is presupposed), would have to make room for the *mechanism* of nature. Now, however, as morality requires nothing but that freedom should only not contradict itself, and that, though unable to understand, we should at least be able to think it, there being no reason why freedom should interfere with the natural mechanism of the same act (if only taken in a different sense), the doctrine of morality may well hold its place, and the doctrine of nature may hold its place too, which would have been impossible, if our critique had not previously taught us our inevitable ignorance with regard to things by themselves, and limited everything, which we are able to *know* theoretically to mere phenomena. The same discussion as to the positive advantage to be derived from the critical principles of pure reason might be repeated with regard to the concept of *God*, and of the *simple nature* of our *soul*; but, for the sake of brevity, I shall pass this by. I am not allowed therefore even to assume, for the sake of the necessary practical employment of my reason, *God*, *freedom*, and *immortality*, if I cannot *deprive* speculative reason of its pretensions to transcendent insights, because reason, in order to arrive at these, must use principles which are intended originally for objects of possible experience only, and which, if in spite of this, they are applied to what cannot be an object of experience, really changes this into a phenomenon, thus rendering all *practical extension* of pure reason impossible. I had therefore to remove *knowledge*, in order to make room for *belief*. For the dogmatism of metaphysic, that is, the presumption that it is possible to achieve anything in metaphysic without a previous criticism of pure reason, is the source of all that unbelief, which is always very dogmatical, and wars against all morality.

If, then, it may not be too difficult to leave a bequest to posterity, in the shape of a systematical metaphysic, carried out according to the critique of pure reason, such a bequest is not to be considered therefore as of little value, whether we regard the improvement which reason receives through the secure method of a science, in place of its groundless groping and uncritical vagaries, or whether we look to the better employment of the time of our enquiring youth, who, if brought up in the ordinary dogmatism, are early encouraged to indulge in easy speculation on things of which they know nothing, and of which they, as little as anybody else, will ever understand anything; neglecting the acquirement of sound knowledge, while bent on the discovery of new metaphysical thoughts and opinions. The greatest benefit however will be, that such a work will enable us to put an end for ever to all objections to morality and religion, according to the Socratic method, namely, by the clearest proof of the ignorance of our opponents. Some kind of metaphysic has always existed, and will always exist, and with it a dialectic of pure reason, as being natural to it. It is therefore the first and most important task of philosophy to deprive metaphysic, once for all, of its pernicious influence, by closing up the sources of its errors.

In spite of these important changes in the whole field of science, and of the losses which speculative reason must suffer in its fancied possessions, all general human interests, and all the advantages which the world hitherto derived from the teachings of pure reason, remain just the same as before. The loss, if any, affects only the *monopoly of the schools*, and by no means the *interests* of *humanity*. I appeal to the staunchest dogmatist, whether the proof of the continued existence of our soul after death, derived from the simplicity of the substance, or that of the freedom of the will, as opposed to the general mechanism of nature, derived from the subtle, but inefficient, distinction between subjective and objective practical necessity, or that of the existence of God, derived from the concept of an *Ens realissimum* (the contingency of the changeable, and the necessity of a prime mover), have ever, after they had been started by the schools, penetrated the public mind, or exercised the slightest influence on its convictions? If this has not been, and in fact could not be so, on account of the unfitness of the ordinary understanding for such subtle speculations; and if, on the contrary, with regard to the first point, the hope of a *future life* has chiefly rested on that peculiar character of human nature, never to be satisfied by what is merely temporal (and insufficient, therefore, for the character of its whole destination); if with regard to the second, the clear consciousness of *freedom* was produced only by the clear exhibition of duties in opposition to all the claims of sensuous desires; and if, lastly, with regard to the third, the belief in a great and wise *Author of the world* has been supported entirely by the wonderful beauty, order, and providence, everywhere displayed in nature, then this possession remains not only undisturbed, but acquires even greater authority, because the schools have now been taught, not to claim for themselves any higher or fuller insight on a point which concerns general human interests, than what is equally within the reach of the great mass of men, and to confine themselves to the elaboration of these universally comprehensible, and, for moral purposes, quite sufficient proofs. The change therefore affects the arrogant pretensions of schools only, which would fain be considered as the only judges and depositaries of such truth (as they are, no doubt, with regard to many other subjects), allowing to the public its use only, and trying to keep the key to themselves, *quod mecum nescit, solus vult scrie videri*. At the same time full satisfaction is given to the more moderate claims of speculative philosophers. They still remain the exclusive depositors of a science, which benefits the masses without their knowing it, namely, the critique of reason. That critique can never become popular, nor does it need to be so, because, if on the one side the public has no understanding of the fine-drawn arguments in support of useful truths, it is not troubled on the other by the equally subtle objections. It is different with the schools which, in the same way as every man who has once risen to the height of speculation, must know both the pro's and the con's and are bound, by means of a careful investigation of the rights of speculative reason, to prevent, once for all, the scandal which, sooner or later, is sure to be caused even to the masses, by the quarrels in which metaphysicians (and as such, theologians also) become involved, if ignorant of our critique, and by which their doctrine becomes in the end entirely perverted. Thus, and thus alone, can the very root be cut off of *materialism, fatalism, atheism, free-thinking, unbelief, fanaticism* and *superstition*, which may become universally injurious, and finally of *idealism* and *scepticism* also, which are dangerous rather to the schools, and can scarcely ever penetrate into the public. If governments think proper ever to interfere with the affairs of the learned, it would be far more consistent with their wise regard for science as well as for *society*, to favour the freedom of such a criticism by which alone the labours of reason can be established on a firm footing, than to support the ridiculous despotism of the schools, which raise a loud clamour of public danger, whenever the cobwebs are swept away of which the public has never taken the slightest notice, and the loss of which it can never therefore perceive.

Our critique is not opposed to the *dogmatical procedure* of reason, as a science of pure knowledge (for this must always be dogmatical, that is, derive its proof from sure principles *a priori*), but to dogmatism only, that is, to the presumption that it is possible to make any progress with pure (philosophical) knowledge, consisting of concepts, and guided by principles, such as reason has long been in the habit of employing, without first enquiring in what way, and by what right, it has come possessed of them. Dogmatism is therefore the dogmatical procedure of pure reason, *without a previous criticism of its own powers*; and our opposition to this is not intended to defend either that loquacious shallowness which arrogates to itself the good name of popularity, much less that scepticism which makes short work with the whole of metaphysic. On the contrary, our critique is meant to form a necessary preparation in support of a thoroughly scientific system of metaphysic, which must necessarily be carried our dogmatically and strictly systematically, so as to satisfy of all the demands, not so much of the public at large, as of the schools, this being an indispensable condition, as it has undertaken to carry out its work entirely *a priori*, and thus to the complete satisfaction of speculative reason. In the execution of this plan, as traced out by the critique, that is, in a future system of metaphysic, we shall have to follow in the strict method of the celebrated Wolff,[6] the greatest of all dogmatic philosopher, who first showed (and by his example called forth, in Germany, that spirit of thoroughness, which is not yet extinct) how the secure method of a science could be attained only by a legitimate establishment of principles, a clear definition of concepts, an attempt at strictness of proof, and an avoidance of all bold combinations in concluding. He was therefore most eminently qualified to raise metaphysic to the dignity of a science, if it had only occurred to him, by criticism of the organum, namely, of pure reason itself, first to prepare his field—an omission to be ascribed, not so much to himself as to the dogmatical spirit of his age, and with regard to which the philosophers of his own, as well as of all previous times, have no right to reproach each other. Those who reject, at the same time, the method of Wolff, and the procedure of the critique of pure reason, can have no other aim but shake off the fetters of science altogether, and thus to change work into play, conviction into opinion, and philosophy into philodoxy.

With regard to this second edition, I have tried, as was but fair, to do all I could in order to remove, as far as

---

6. Christian Wolff (1679-1754).

possible, the difficulties and obscurities which, not perhaps without my fault, have misled even acute thinkers in judging of my book. In the propositions themselves, and their proofs, likewise in the form and completeness of the whole plan, I have found nothing to alter, which is due partly to the long-continued examination to which I had subjected them, before submitting them to the public, and partly to the nature of the subject itself. For pure speculative reason is so constituted that it forms a true organism, in which everything is *organic*, the whole being there for the sake of every part, and every part for the sake of the whole, so that the smallest imperfection, whether a fault or a deficiency, must inevitably betray itself in use. I venture to hope that this system will maintain itself unchanged for the future also. It is not self-conceit which justifies me in this confidence, but the experimental evidence produced by the identity of the result, whether we proceed progressively from the smallest elements to the whole of pure reason, or retrogressively from the whole (for this also is given by the practical objects of reason) to every single part; the fact being, that an attempt at altering even the smallest item produces at once contradictions, not only in the system, but in human reason in general. With regard to the *style*, however, much remains to be done; and for that purpose, I have endeavoured to introduce several improvements into this second edition, which are intended to remove, first, misapprehensions in the Aesthetic, especially with regard to the concept of time: secondly, obscurities in the deduction of the concepts of the understanding: thirdly, a supposed want of sufficient evidence, in proving the propositions of the pure understanding: fourthly, the false interpretation put on the paralogisms with which we charged rational psychology. To this point do the changes of style and representation[7] extend, and no further. Time was too short for doing more, nor did I, with regard to the rest, meet with any misapprehensions on the part of competent and impartial judges. These, even though I must not name them with

---

7. The only thing which might be called an addition, though in the method of proof only, is the new refutation of *psychological idealism*, and the strict (and as I believe the only possible) proof of the objective reality of external phenomena. That idealism may be considered entirely innocent with respect to the essential aims of metaphysic (though it is not so in reality), yet it remains a scandal to philosophy, and to human reason in general, that we should have to accept the existence of things without us (from which we derive the whole material of knowledge for our own internal sense) on faith only, unable to meet with any satisfactory proof an opponent, who is pleased to doubt it. It will probably be urged against this proof that, after all, I am immediately conscious of that only which is within me, that is, of my *representation* of external things, and that consequently it must still remain uncertain whether there be outside me anything corresponding to it or not. But by internal *experience* I am conscious of *my existence in time* (consequently also, of this determinability in time); and this is more than to be conscious of my representation only, and yet identical with the *empirical consciousness of my existence*, which can be itself determined only by something connected with my existence, yet outside me. This consciousness of my existence in time is therefore connected as identical with the consciousness of relation to something *outside* me; so that it is experience, and

that praise which is due to them, will easily perceive in the proper place, that I have paid careful attention to their remarks.

---

not fiction, sense, and not imagination, which indissolubly connects the external with my internal sense. The external sense is by itself relation of intuition to something real outside me; and its real, in contradistinction to a purely imaginary character, rests entirely on its being indissolubly connected with internal experience, as being the condition of its possibility. This is what happens here. If with the *intellectual consciousness* of my existence in the representation, *I am*, which accompanies all my judgments and all acts of my understanding, I could at the same time connect determination of that existence of mine by means of *intellectual intuition*, then that determination would not require the consciousness of relation to something outside me. But although that intellectual consciousness comes first, the inner intuition, in which alone any existence can be determined, is sensuous and dependent on the condition of time; and that determination again, and therefore internal experience itself, depends on something permanent which is not within me, consequently on something outside me only, to which I must consider myself as standing in a certain relation. Hence the reality of the external sense in necessarily connected, in order to make experience possible at all, with the reality of the internal sense; that is, I am conscious, with the same certainty, that there are things outside me which have a reference to my sense, as that I exist myself in time. In order to ascertain to what given intuitions objects outside me really correspond (these intuitions belonging to the *external sense*, and not to the faculty imagination), we must in each single case apply the rules according to which experience in general (even internal) is distinguished from imaginations, the proposition that there really is an external experience being

I have observed with pleasure and thankfulness in various publications (containing either reviews or separate essays) that the spirit of thoroughness is not yet dead in Germany, but has only been silenced for a short time by the clamour of a fashionable and pretentious licence of thought, and that the difficulies which beset the thorny path of my critique, which is to lead to a truly scientific and as, such, permanent, and therefore most necessary, science of pure reason, have not discouraged bold and clear heads from mastering my book. To these excellent men, who so happily blend thorough knowledge with a talent for lucid exposition (to which I can lay no claim), I leave the task of bringing my, in that respect far from perfect, work to greater perfection. There is no danger of its being refuted, though there is of its being misunderstood. For my own part, I cannot henceforth enter

---

always taken for grated. It may be well to add here the remark that *the representation of something permanent* in existence is not the same as a *permanent representation*; for this (the representation of something permanent in existence) can change and alternate, as all our representations, even those of matter, and may yet refer to something permanent, which must therefore be something external, and different from all my representations, the *existence* of which is necessarily involved in the *determination* of my own existence, and constitutes with it but one experience, which could never take place internally, unless (in part) it were external also. The *how* admits here of as little explanation as the permanent in time in general, the co-existence of which with the variable produces the concept of change.

on controversies, though I shall carefully attend to all hints, whether from friends or opponents, in order to utilize them in a future elaboration of the whole system, according to the plan traced our in this *propaedeutic*. As during these labours I have advanced pretty far in years (this very month, into my sixty-forth year), I must be careful in spending my time, if I am to carry out my plan, of furnishing a metaphysic of nature, and a metaphysic of morals, in confirmation of the truth of my critique both of speculative and of practical reason, and must leave the elucidation of such obscurities as could at first be hardly avoided in such a work, and likewise the defence of the whole, to those excellent men who have made it their own. At single points every philosophical treatise may be pricked (for it cannot be armed at all points, like a mathematical one), while yet the organic structure of the system, considered as a whole, has not therefore to apprehend the slightest danger. Few only have the pliability of intellect to take in the whole of a system, if it is new; still fewer have an inclination for it, because they dislike every innovation. If we take single passages out of their connection, and contrast them with each other, it is easy to pick out apparent contradictions, particularly in a work written with all the freedom of a running speech. In the eyes of those who rely on the judgment of others, such contradictions may throw and unfavourable light on any work; but they are easily removed, if we ourselves have once grasped the idea of the whole. And, if a theory possesses stability in itself, then this action and reaction of praise and blame, which at first seemed so dangerous, serve only in time to rub off its superficial inequalities; nay, secure to it, in a short time, the requisite elegance also, if only men of insight, impartiality, and true popularity will devote themselves to its study.

Of the distinction between Analytical and Synthetical Judgements

In all judgments in which there is a relation between subject and predicate (I speak of affirmative judgments only, the application to negative ones being easy), that relation can be of two kinds. Either the predicate B belongs to the subject A as something contained (though covertly) in the concept A; or B lies outside the sphere of the concept A, though somehow connected with it. In the former case I call the judgments (affirmative) are therefore those in which the connection of the predicate with the subject is conceived through identity, may be called synthetical. The former might be called illustrating, the latter expanding judgments, because in the former nothing is added by the predicate to the concept of the subject, but the concept is only divided into its constituent concepts which were always conceived as existing within it, though confusedly; while the latter add to the concept of the subject a predicate not conceived as existing within it, and not to be extracted from it by any process of mere analysis. If I say, for instance, All bodies are extended, this is an analytical judgment. I need not go beyond the concept connected with the name of body, in order to find that extension is connected with it. I have only to analyse that concept and become conscious of the manifold elements always contained in it, in order to find that predicate. This is therefore an analytical judgment. But if I say, all bodies are heavy, the predicate is something quite different from what I think as the mere concept of body. The addition of such a predicate gives us a synthetical judgment.

Empirical judgments, as such, are all synthetical, for it would be absurd to found an analytical judgment on experience, because, in order to form such a judgment, I need not at all step out of my concept, or appeal to the testimony of experience. That a body is extended, is a proposition perfectly certain *a priori*, and not an empirical judgement. For, before I call in experience, I am already in possession of all the conditions of my judgment in the concept of body itself. I have only to draw out from it, according to the principle of contradiction, the required predicate, and I thus become conscious, at the same time, of the necessity of judgment, which experience could never teach me. But, though I do not include the predicate of gravity in the general concept of body, that concept, nevertheless, indicates an object of experience through one of its parts: so that I may add other parts also of the same experience, besides those which belonged to the former concept. I may, first, by an analytical process, realize the concept of body, through the predicates of extension, impermeability, form, etc., all of which are contained in it. Afterwards I expand my knowledge, and looking back the experience from which my concept of body was abstracted, I find gravity always connected with the before-mentioned predicates, and therefore I add it synthetically to that concept as a predicate. It is, therefore, experience on which the possibility of the synthesis of the predicate of gravity with the concept of body is founded: because both concepts, though neither of them is contained in the other, belong to each other, though accidentally only, as parts of a whole, namely, of experience, which is itself a synthetical connection of intuitions.

In synthetical judgements *a priori*, however, that help is entirely wanting. If I want to go beyond the concept A in order to find another concept B connected with it, where is there anything on which I may rest and through which a synthesis might become possible, considering that I cannot have the advantage of looking about in the field of experience? Take the proposition that all which happens has its cause. In the concept of something that happens I no doubt conceive of something existing preceded by time, and from this certain analytical judgments may be deducted. But the concept of cause is entirely outside that concept, and indicates something different from that which happens, and is by no means contained in that representation. How can I venture then to predicate of that which happens something totally different from it, and to represent the concept of cause, though not contained in it, as belonging to it, and belonging to it by necessity? What is here the unknown *x*, on which the understanding may rest in order to find beyond the concept A a foreign predicate B, which nevertheless is believed to be connected with it? It cannot be experience, because the proposition that all which happens has its cause represents this second predicate as added to the subject not only with greater generality than experience can ever supply, but also with a character of necessity, and therefore purely *a priori*, and based on concepts. All our speculative knowledge *a priori* aims at and rests on such synthical, *i.e.* expending propositions, for the analytical are no doubt very important and necessary, yet only in order to arrive at that clearness of concepts which is requisite for a safe and wide synthesis, serving as a really new addition to what we possess already (and always the same).

Transcendental exposition of the concept of space

I understand by transcendental *exposition*, the explanation of a concept, as of a principle by which the possibility of other synthetical cognitions *a priori* can be understood. For this purpose it is necessary (1) That such cognitions really do flow from the given concept. (2) That they are possible only under the pre-supposition of a given mode of explanation of such concept.

Geometry is a science which determines the properties of space synthetically, and yet *a priori*. What then must be the representation of space, to render such a knowledge of it possible? It must be originally intuitive; for it is impossible from a mere concept to deduce propositions which go beyond that concept, as we do in geometry. That intuition, however, must be *a priori*, that is, it must exist within us before any perception of the object, and must therefore be pure, not empirical intuition. For all geometrical propositions are apodictic, that is, connected with the consciousness of their necessity, as for instance the proposition, that space has only three dimension; and such propositions cannot be empirical judgments, nor conclusions from them.

How then can an external intuition dwell in the mind anterior to the objects themselves, and in which the concept of objects can be determined *a priori*? Evidently not otherwise than so far as it has its seat in the subject only, as the formal condition under which the subject is affected by the objects and thereby is receiving an *immediate representation*, that is, *intuition* of them; therefore as a form of the external sense in general.

It is therefore by our explanation only that the *possibility* of *geometry* as a synthetical science *a priori* becomes intelligible. Every other explanation, which fails to account of this possibility, can best be distinguished from our own by that criterion, although it may seems to have some similarity with it.

Transcendental exposition of the concept of time

To say that time is infinite means no more than that every definite quantity of time is possible only by limitations of one time which forms the foundation of all times. The original representation of time must therefore be given as unlimited. But when the parts themselves and every quantity of an object can be represented as determined by limitation only, the whole representation cannot be given by concepts (for in that case the partial representations come first), but it must be founded on immediate intuition.

The concept of change, and with it the concept of motion (as change of place), is possible only through and

CRITIQUE OF PURE REASON 81

in the representation of time; and that, if this representation were not intuitive (internal) *a priori*, no concept, whatever it be, could make us understand the possibility of a change, that is, of a connection of contradictorily opposed predicates (for instance, the being and not-being of one and the same thing in one and the same place) in one and the same object. It is only time that both contradictorily opposed determinations can be met with in the same object, that is, one after the other. Our concept of time, therefore, exhibits the possibility of as many synthetical cognitions *a priori* as are found in the general doctrine of motion, which is very rich in them.

The principle of the synthetical unity of Apperception is the highest principle of all employment of the understanding

The highest principle of the possibility of all intuition, in relation to sensibility, was, according to the transcendental Aesthetic, that all the manifold in it should subject to the formal conditions of space and time. The highest principle of the same possibility in relation to the understanding is, that all the manifold in intuition must be subject to the conditions of the original synthetical unity of apperception.[8]

---

8. Space and time, and all portions thereof, are *intuitions*, and consequently single representations with the manifold of their content. They are not, therefore, mere concepts, through which the same consciousness, as existing in many representations, but intuitions through which many representations are brought

All the manifold representations of intuition, so far as they are given us, are subject to the former, so far as they must admit of being connected in one consciousness, to the latter; and without that nothing can be thought or known by them, because the given representations would not share the act of appreciation (I think) in common, and could not be comprehended in one self-consciousness.

The *understanding* in its most general sense is the faculty of *congnitions*. These consist in a definite relation of given representations to an object; and an *object* is that in the concept of which the manifold of a given intuition is connected. All such connection of representations requires of course the unity of consciousness in their sysnthesis: consequently the unity of consciousness is that which alone constitutes the relation of representations to an object, that is, their objective validity, and consequently their becoming congnitions, so that the very possibility of the understanding depends on it.

The first pure cognition of the understanding, therefore, on which all the rest of its employment is founded, and which at the same time is entirely independent of all conditions of sensuous intuition, is this very principle of the original synthetical unity of apperception. Space, the mere form of external sensuous

---

to us, as contained in one and in its consciousness; this latter, therefore, is compounded, and those intuitions represent the unity of consciousness as *synthetical*, but yet as primitive. This character of singleness in them is practically of great importance.

intuition, is not yet cognition: it only supplies the manifold of intuition *a priori* for a possible congnition. In order to know anything in space, for instance, a line, I must draw it, and produce synthetically certain connection of the manifold that is given, so that the unity of that act is at the same time the unity of the consciousness (in the concept of a line), and (so that) an object (a determinate space) is then only known for the first time. The synthetical unity of consciousness is, therefore, an objective condition of all knowledge; a condition, not necessary for myself only, in order to know an object, but one to which each intuition must be subject, in order to become an object for me, because the manifold could not become connected in one consciousness in any other way, and without such a synthesis.

Not doubt, that proposition, as I said before, is itself analytical, though it makes synthetical unity a condition of all thought, for it really says no more than that all representations in any given intuition must be subject to the condition under which alone I can ascribe them as my representations, to the identical self, and therefore comprehend them, as synthetically connected, in one apperception through the general expression, *I think*.

And yet this need not be a principle for every possible understanding, but only for that which gives nothing manifold through its pure apperception in the representation, *I am*. An understanding which through its self-consciousness could give the manifold of intuition, and by whose representation the objects of that representation should at the same time exist, which would not require a special act of the synthesis of the manifold for the unity of its consciousness, while the human understanding, which possesses the power of thought only, but not of intuition, requires such an act. To the human understanding that first principle is so indispensable that it really cannot form the least concept of any other possible understanding, whether it be intuitive by itself, or possessed of a sensuous intuition, different from that in space and time.

What is the objective unity of self-consciousness?

The transcendental *unity* of apperception connects all the manifold given in an intuition into a concept of an object. It is therefore called *objective*, and must be distinguished from the subjective unity of consciousness, which is a form of the *internal sense*, by which the manifold of intuition is empirically given, to be thus connected. Whether I can become *empirically* conscious of the manifold, as either simultaneous or successive, depends on circumstances, or empirical conditions. The empirical unity of consciousness, therefore, though the association of representations, is itself phenomenal and wholly contingent, while the pure form of intuition in time, merely, is subject to the original unity of the consciousness, through the necessary relation only of the manifold of intuition to the one, *I think*—that is, through the pure synthesis of the understanding, which forms the *a priori* ground of the empirical synthesis. That unity alone is, therefore, valid objectively; the empirical unity of apperception, which we do not consider here, and which is only derived from the former, under given conditions *in concreto*, has subjective validity only. One man connects the representation of a word with one thing, another with another, and the unity of consciousness, with regard to what is empirical, is not necessary nor universally valid with reference to that which is given.

Transcendental Idealism as the key to the solution of the cosmological dialectic

It has been sufficiently proved in the transcendental Aesthetic that everything which is perceived in space and time, therefore all objects of an experience possible to us, are nothing but phenomena, that is, mere representations which, such as they are represented, namely, as extended beings, or series of changes, have no independent existence outside our thoughts. This system I call *Transcendental Idealism*. I have sometimes called it *formal* idealism also, in order to distinguish it from the *material* or common idealism which doubts or denies the very existence of external things. In some cases it seems advisable to use these terms rather than those in the text, in order to prevent all misunderstanding. Transcendental realism changes these modifications of our sensibility into self-subsistent things, that is, it changes *mere representations* into things by themselves.

It would be unfair to ask us to adopt that long-decried empirical idealism which, while it admits the independent reality of space, denies the existence of extended beings in it, or at all events considers it as doubtful and does not admit that there is in this respect a sufficiently established difference between dream and reality. It sees no difficulty with regard to the phenomena of the internal sense in time, being real things; nay, it even maintains that this internal experience alone sufficiently proves the real existence of its object (by itself), with all the determinations in time.

Our own transcendental idealism, on the contrary, allows that the objects of external intuition may be real, as they are perceived in space, and likewise all changes in time, as they are represented by the internal sense. For as space itself is a form of that intuition which we call external, and as there would be no empirical representation at all, unless there were objects in space, we can and must admit the extended being in it as real; and the same applies to time. Space itself, however, as well as time, and with them all phenomena, are not things by themselves, but representations, and cannot exist outside our mind; and even the internal sensuous intuition of our mind (as an object of consciousness) which is represented as determined by the succession of different states in time, is not a real self, as it exists by itself, or what is called the transcendental subject, but a phenomenon only, given to the sensibility of this to us unknown being. It cannot be admitted that this internal phenomenon exists as a thing by itself, because it is under the condition of time, which can never be the determination of anything by itself. In space and time, however, the empirical truth of phenomena is sufficiently established, and kept quite distinct from a dream, if both are properly and completely connected together in experience, according to empirical laws.

The objects of experience are therefore *never given by themselves*, but in our experience only, and do not exist outside it. That there may be inhabitants in the moon, though no man has ever seen them, must be admitted, but it means no more than that, in the possible programme of our experience, we may meet with them; for everything is real that hangs together with a perception, according to the laws of empirical progress. They are therefore real, if they are empirically connected with any real consciousness, although they are not therefore real by themselves, that is, apart from that progress for experience.

Nothing is really given to us but perception, and the empirical progress from this to other possible perceptions. For by themselves phenomena, as mere representations, are real in perception only, which itself is nothing but the reality of an empirical representation, that is, phenomenal appearance. To call a phenomenon a real thing, before it is perceived, means either, that in the progress of experience we must meet with such a perception, or it means nothing. For that it existed by itself, without any reference to our senses and possible experience, might no doubt be said when we speak of a thing by itself. We here are speaking, however, of a phenomenon only in space and time, which are not determinations of things by themselves, but only of our sensibility. Hence that which exists in them (phenomena) is not something by itself, but consists in representations only, which, unless they are given in us (in perception), exist nowhere.

The faculty of sensuous intuition is really some kind of receptivity only, according to which we are affected in a certain way by representations the mutual relation of which is a pure intuition of space and time (mere forms of our sensibility), and which, if they are connected and determined in that relation of space and time, according to the laws of the unity of experience, are called objects. The non-sensuous cause of these representations is entirely unknown to us, and we can never perceive it as an object, for such a cause would have to be represented neither in space nor in time, which are conditions of sensuous representations only, and without which we cannot conceive any intuition. We may, however, call that purely intelligible cause of phenomena in general, the transcendental object, in order that we may have something which corresponds to sensibility as a kind of receptivity. We may ascribe to that transcendental object the whole extent and connection of all our possible perceptions, and we may say that it is given by itself antecedently to all experience. Phenomena, however, are given accordingly, not by themselves, but in experience only, because they are mere representations which as perceptions only, signify a real object, provided that the perception is connected with all others, according to the rules of unity in experience. Thus we may say that the real things of time past are given in the transcendental object of experience, but they only are objects to me, and real in time past, on the supposition that I conceive that a regressive series of possible perceptions (whether by the light of history, or by the vestiges of causes and effects), in one word, the course of the world, leads, according to empirical laws, to a past series of time, as a condition of the present time. It is therefore represented as real, not by itself, but in connection with a possible experience, so that all past events from time immemorial and before my own existence mean after all nothing but the possibility of an extension of the chain of experience, beginning with present perception and leading upwards to the conditions which determine it in time.

If, therefore, I represent to myself all existing objects of the senses, at all times and in all spaces, I do not place them before experience into space and time, but the whole representation is nothing but the idea of a possible experience, in its absolute completeness. In that alone those objects (which are nothing but mere representations) are given; and if we say that they exist before my whole experience, this only means that they exist in that part of experience to which, starting from perception, I have first to advance. The cause of empirical conditions of that progress, and consequently with what members, or how far I may meet with certain members in that regressus, is transcendental, and therefore entirely unknown to me. But that cause does not concern us, but only the rule of progress of experience, in which objects, namely phenomena, are given to me. In the end it is just the same whether I say, that in the empirical progress in space I may meet with stars a hundred times more distant that the most distant which I see, or whether I say that such stars are perhaps to be met with in space, though no human being did ever or will ever see them. For though, as things by themselves, they might be given without any relation to possible experience, they are nothing to me, and therefore no objects, unless they can be comprehended in the series of the empirical regressus. Only in another relation, when namely these phenomena are meant to be used for the cosmological idea of an absolute whole, and when we have to deal with a question that goes beyond the limits of possible experience, the distinction of the mode in which the reality of those objects of the senses is taken becomes of importance, in order to guard against a deceptive error that would inevitably arise from a misinterpretation of our own empirical concepts.

Of the empirical use of the regulative principle of reason with regard to all cosmological ideas

No transcendental use, as we have shown on several occasions, can be made of the concepts either of the understanding or of reason; and the absolute totality of the series of conditions in the world of sense is due entirely to a transcendental use of reason, which demands this unconditioned completeness from what presupposes as a thing by itself. As no such thing is contained in the world of sense, we can never speak again of the absolute quantity of different series in it, whether they be limited or in themselves unlimited; but the question can only be, how far, in the empirical regressus, we may go back in tracing experience to its conditions, in order to stop, according to the rule of reason, at no other answer of its questions but such as is in accordance with the object.

What therefore remains to us is only the *validity of the principle of reason*, as a rule for the continuation and for the extent of a possible experience, after its invalidity, as a constitutive principle of things by themselves, has been sufficiently established. If we have clearly established that invalidity, the conflict of reason with itself will be entirely finished, because not only has the illusion which led to that conflict been removed through critical analysis but in its place the sense in which reason agrees with itself, and the misapprehension of which was the only cause of conflict, has been clearly exhibited, and a principle formerly *dialectical* changed into a doctrinal one. In fact, if that principle, according to its subjective meaning, can be proved fit to determine the greatest possible use of the understanding in experience, as adequate to its objects, this would be the same as if it determined, as an axiom (which is impossible from pure reason), the objects themselves *a priroi*; for this also could not, with reference to the object of experience, exercise a greater influence on the extension and correction of our knowledge, than proving itself efficient in the most extensive use of our understanding as applied to experience.

Solution of the cosmological idea of the totality of the composition of the phenomena in a universe

Here, as well as in the other cosmological problems, the regulative principle of reason is founded on the proposition that, in the empirical regressus, *no experience of an absolute limit*, that is of any condition as such, which *empirically* is *absolutely unconditioned*, can exist. The ground of this is that such an experience would contain a limitation of phenomena by nothing or by the void, on which the continued regressus by means of experience must abut; and this is impossible.

This proposition, which says that in an empirical

regressus I can only arrive at the condition which itself must be considered empirically conditioned, contains the rule *in terminis*, that however far I may have reached in the ascending series, I must always enquire for a still higher member of that series, whether it be known to me by experience or not.

For the solution, therefore, of the first cosmological problem, nothing more is wanted than to determine whether, in the regressus to the unconditioned extension of the universe (in time and in space), this nowhere limited ascent is to be called a regressus *in infinitum*, or a *regressus in indefinitum*.

The mere general representation of the series of all past states of the world, and of the things which exist together in space, is itself nothing but a possible empirical regressus, which I represent to myself, though as yet as indefinite, and through which alone the concept of such a series of conditions of the perception given to me can arise.[9] Now the universe exists for me as a concept only, and never (as a whole) as an intuition. Hence I cannot from its quantity conclude the quantity of the regressus, and determine the one by the other; but I must first frame to myself a concept of the quantity of the world through the

---

9. This cosmical series can therefore be neither greater nor smaller than the possible empirical regressus on which alone its concept rests. And as this can give neither a definite infinite, nor a definite finite (absolutely limited), it becomes clear that we cannot accept the quantity of the world, either as finite or as infinite, because the regressus (by which it is represented) admits of neither the one nor the other.

quantity of the empirical regressus. Of this, however, I never know anything more than that, empirically, I must go on from every given member of the series of conditions to a higher and more distant member. Hence the quantity of the whole of phenomena is not absolutely determined, and we cannot say therefore that it is *regressus in infinitum*, because this would anticipate the member which the regressus has not yet reached, and represent its numbers as so large that no empirical synthesis could ever reach it. It would therefore (though negatively only) determine the quantity of the world prior to the regressus, which is impossible, because it is not given to me by any intuition (in its totality), so that its quantity cannot be given prior to the regressus. Hence we cannot say anything of the quantity or extension of the world by itself, not even that there is in it a *regressus in infinitum*; but we must look for the concept of its quantity according to the rule that determines the empirical regressus in it. This rule, however, says no more than that, however far we may have got in the series of empirical conditions, we ought never to assume an absolute limit, but subordinate every phenomenon, as conditioned, to another, as its condition, and that we must proceed further to that condition. This is the *regressus in indefinitum*, which, as it fixes no quantity in the object, can clearly enough be distinguished from the *regressus in infinitum*.

I cannot say therefore that, as to time past or as to space, the world is infinite. For such a concept of quantity, as a given infinity, is empirical, and therefore, with reference to the world as an object of the senses, absolutely impossible. Nor shall I say that the regressus, beginning with a given perception, and going on to everything that limits it in a series, both in space and in time past, goes on *in infinitum*, because this would presuppose an infinite quantity of the world. Nor can I say again that it is finite, for the absolute limit is likewise empirically impossible. Hence it follows that I shall not be able to say anything of the whole object of experience (the world of sense), but only of the rule, according to which experience can take place and be continued in accordance with its object.

To the cosmological question, therefore, respecting the quantity of the world, the first and negative answer is, that the world has no first beginning in time, and no extreme limit in space.

For, in the contrary case, the world would be limited by empty time and empty space. As however, as a phenomenon, it cannot, by itself, be either—a phenomenon not being a thing by itself—we should have to admit the perception of a limitation by means of absolute empty time or empty space, by which these limits of the world could be given in a possible experience. Such an experience, however, would be perfectly void of contents, and therefore impossible. Consequently an absolute limit of the world is impossible empirically, and therefore absolutely also.[10]

---

10. It will have been observed that the argument has here been carried on in a very different way from the dogmatical argument, which was presented before, in the antithesis of the first antimony. There we took the world of sense, according to

From this follows at the same time the affirmative answer, that the regressus in the series of the phenomena of the world, intended as a determination of the quantity of the world, goes on *in indefinitum*, which is the same as if to say that the world of sense has no absolute quantity, that the empirical regressus (through which alone it can be given on the side of its conditions) has its own rule, namely, to advance from every member of the series, as conditioned, to a more distant member, whether by our own experience, or by the guidance of history, or through the chain of causes and their effects; and never to dispense with the extension of the possible empirical use of the understanding, this being the proper and really only task of reason and its principles.

We do not prescribe by this a definite empirical regressus advancing without end in a certain class of phenomena; as, for instance, that from a living person one ought always to ascend in a series of ancestors, without ever expecting a first pair, or, in the series of cosmical bodies, without admitting in the end an extremest sun. All that is demanded is a progressus from phenomena to phenomena, even if they should not furnish us with a real perception (if it is too weak in degree to become experience in our consciousness), because even thus they belong to a possible experience.

---

the common and dogmatical view, as a thing given by itself, in its totality, before any regressus: and we had denied to it, if it did not occupy all time and all space, and place at all in both. Hence the conclusion also was different from what it is here, for it went to the real infinity of the world.

Every beginning is in time, and every limit of extension in space. Space and time, however, exist in the world of sense only. Hence phenomena only are limited *in the world* conditionally; the *world* itself, however, is limited neither conditionally nor unconditionally.

For the same reason, and because the world can never be given *complete*, and even the series of conditions of something given as conditioned cannot, as a cosmical series, be given as complete, the concept of the quantity of the world can be given through the regressus only, and not before it in any collective intuition. That regressus, however, consists only in the determining of the quantity, and does not give, therefore, any definite concept, nor the concept of any quantity which, with regard to a certain measure, could be called infinite. It does not therefore proceed to the infinite (as if given), but only into an indefinite distance, in order to give a quantity (of experience) which has first to be realized by the very regressus.

Solution of the cosmological idea of the totality of the division of a whole given in intuition

If I divide a whole, given in intuition, I proceed from the conditioned to the conditions of its possibility. The division of the parts (*subdivisio* or *decompositio*) is a regressus in the series of those conditions. The absolute totality of this series could only be given, if the regressus could reach the simple parts. But if all parts in a continuously progressing decomposition are always divisible again, then the division, that is, the regressus from the conditioned to its conditions, goes on *in infinitum*; because the conditions (the parts) are contained in the conditioned itself, and as that is given as complete in an intuition enclosed within limits, are all given with it. The regressus must therefore not be called a *regressus in indefinitum*, such as was alone allowed by the former cosmological idea, where from the conditioned we had to proceed to conditions outside it, and therefore not given at the same time through it, but first to be added in the empirical regressus. It is not allowed, however, even in the case of a whole that is divisible *in infinitum*, to say, that it consists of infinitely many parts. For although all parts are contained in the intuition of the whole, yet the whole division is not contained in it, because it consists in the continuous decomposition, or in the regressus itself, which first makes that series real. A this regressus is infinite, all members (parts) at which it arrives are contained, no doubt, in the given whole as aggregates; but not so the whole series of the division, which is successively infinite and never complete, and cannot, therefore, represent an infinite number, or any comprehension of it as a whole.

It is easy to apply this remark to space. Every space, perceived within its limits, is such a whole the parts of which, in spite of all decomposition, are always spaces again, and therefore divisible *in infinitum*.

From this follows, quite naturally, the second application to an external phenomenon, enclosed within its limits (body). The divisibility of this is founded on the divisibility of space, which constitutes the possibility of the body, as an extended whole. This is therefore divisible *in infinitum*, without consisting, however, of an infinite number of parts.

It might seem indeed, as a body must be represented as a substance in space, that, with regard to the law of the divisibility of space, it might differ from it, for we might possibly concede, that in the latter case decomposition could never do away with all composition, because in that case all space, which besides has nothing independent of its own, would cease to be (which is impossible), while, even if all composition of matter should be done away with in thought, it would not seem compatible with the concept of a substance that nothing should remain of it, because substance is meant to be the subject of all composition, and ought to remain in its elements, although their connection in space, by which they become a body, should have been removed. But, what applies to a thing by itself, represented by a pure concept of the under-standing, does not apply to what is called a substance, as a phenomenon. This is not an absolute subject, but only a permanent image of sensibility, nothing in fact but intuition, in which nothing unconditioned can ever be met with.

But although this rule of the progress *in infinitum* applies without any doubt to the subdivision of a phenomenon, as a mere occupant of space, it does not apply to the number of the parts, separated already in a certain way in a given whole, which thus constitute a *quantum discretum*. To suppose that in every organized whole every part is again organized, and that by thus dissecting the parts *in infinitum* we should meet again and again with new organized parts, in fact that the whole is organized *in infinitum*, is a thought difficult to think, though it is possible to think that the parts of matter decomposed *in infinitum* might become organized. For the infinity of the division of a given phenomenon in space is founded simply on this, that by it *divisibility* only, that is, and entirely indefinite number of parts, is given, while the parts themselves can only be given and determined through the subdivision, in short, that the whole is not itself already divided. Thus the division can determine a number in it, which goes so far as we like to go, in the regressus of a division. In an organic body, on the contrary, organized *in infinitum* the whole is by that very concept represented as divided, and a number of parts, definite in itself, and yet infinite, is found in it, before every regressus of division. This would be self-contradictory, because we should have to consider this infinite convolute as a never-to-be-completed series (infinite), and yet as complete in its (organized) compre-hension. Infinite division takes the phenomenon only as a *quantum continuum*, and is inseparable from the occupation of space, because in this very occupation lies the ground of endless divisibility. But as soon as anything is taken as a *quantum discretum*, the number of units in it is determined, and therefore at all times equal to a certain number. How far the organization in an organized body may go, experience alone can show us; but though it never arrived with certainty at any unorganized part, they would still have to be admitted as lying within possible experience. It is different with the transcendental division of a phenomenon. How far that may extend is not a matter of experience, but a principle of reason, which never allows us to consider the empirical regressus in the decomposition of extended bodies, according to the nature of these phenomena, as at any time absolutely competed.

Concluding remarks of the solutions of the transcendental-mathematical ideas, and preliminary remark for the solution of the transcendental-dynamical ideas

When exhibiting in tabular from the antinomy of pure reason, through all the transcendental ideas, and indicating the ground of the conflict and the only means of removing it, by declaring both contradictory statements as false, we always represented the conditions as belonging to that which they conditioned, according to relations of space and time, this being the ordinary supposition of the common understanding, and in fact the source from which that conflict arose. In that respect all dialectical representations of the totality in a series of conditions of something given as conditioned were always of the *same character*. It was always a series in which the condition was connected with the conditioned, as members of the same series, both being thus *homogeneous*. In such a series the regressus was never conceived as completed, or, if that had to be done, one of the members, being in itself conditioned, had wrongly to be accepted as the first, and therefore as unconditioned. If not always the object, that is, the conditioned, yet the series of its conditions were always considered according to quantity only, and then the difficulty arose (which could not be removed by any compromise, but only by cutting the knot), that reason made it either *too long* or *too short* for the understanding, which could in neither case come up to the idea.

But in this we have overlooked of the understanding, which reason tries to raise into ideas. Two of them, according to the above table of categories, imply a *mathematical*, the remaining two a *dynamical* synthesis of phenomena. Hitherto this overlooking was of no great importance, because, in the general representation of all transcendental ideas, we always remained under *phenomenal* conditions, and with regard to the two transcendental-mathematical ideas also, we had to do with no object but the phenomenal only. Now, however, as we have come to consider the *dynamical* concepts of the understanding, so far as they should be rendered adequate to the idea of reason, that distinction becomes important, and opens to us an entirely new insight into the character of the suit in which reason is implicated. That suit had before been dismissed, as resting on both sides on wrong presuppositions. Now, however, as there seems to be in the dynamical antinomy such a presupposition as may be compatible with the pretensions of reason, and as the judge himself supplies perhaps the deficiency of legal grounds, which had been misunderstood on both sides, the suit may possibly be adjusted, from this point of view, to the satisfaction of both parties, which was impossible in the conflict of the mathematical antinomy.

If we merely look to the extension of the series of

conditions, and whether they are adequate to the idea, or whether the idea is too large or too small for them, the series are no doubt all homogeneous. But the concept of the understanding on which these ideas are founded contains either a *synthesis* of the *homogeneous* only (which is presupposed in the composition as well as the decomposition of every quantity), or of the heterogeneous also, which must at least be admitted as possible in the dynamical synthesis, both in a causal connection, and in the connection of the necessary with the contingent.

Thus it happens that none but sensuous conditions can enter into the mathematical connection of the series of phenomena, that is, conditions which themselves are part of the series, while the *dynamical* series of sensuous conditions admits also of a *heterogeneous* condition, which is not a part of the series, but as merely intelligible, outside it; so that a certain satisfaction is given to reason by the unconditioned being placed before the phenomena, without disturbing the series of the phenomena, which must always be conditioned, or breaking it off, contrary to the principles of the understanding.

Owing to the dynamical ideas admitting of a condition of the phenomena outside their series, that is, a condition which itself is not phenomenon, something aries which is totally different from the result of the antinomy. The result of that antinomy was, that both the contradictory dialectical statements had to be declared false. The throughout conditioned character, however, of the dynamical series, which is inseparable from them as phenomena, if connected with the empirically unconditioned, but at the same time *not sensuous* condition, may give satisfaction to the *understanding* on one, and *reason* on the other side,[11] because the dialectical arguments which, in some way or other, required unconditioned totality in mere phenomena, vanish; while the proposition of reason, if thus amended, may *both be true*. This cannot be the case with the cosmological ideas, which refer only to a mathematically unconditioned unity, because with them no condition can be found in the series of phenomena which is not itself a phenomenon, and as such constitutes one of the links of the series.

Solution of the cosmological ideas with regard to the totality of the derivation of cosmical events from their causes

We can conceive two kinds of causality only with reference to events, causality either of *nature* or of *freedom*. The former is the connection of one state in the world of sense with a preceding state, on which it follows according to a rule. As the causality of phenomena

---

11. The understanding admits of no condition *among phenomena*, which should itself be empirically unconditioned. But if we might conceive an *intelligible condition*, that is to say, a condition, not belonging itself as a link to the series of phenomena, of something conditioned (as a phenomenon) without in the least interrupting the series of empirical conditions, such a condition might be admitted as *empirically unconditioned*, without interfering with the empirical continuous regressus.

depends on conditions of time, and as the preceding state, if it had always existed, could not have produced an effect, which first takes place in time, it follows that the causality of the cause of that which happens or arises must, according to the principle of the understanding, have itself arisen and require a cause.

By freedom, on the contrary, in its cosmological meaning, I understand the faculty of beginning a state *spontaneously*. Its causality, therefore, does not depend, according to the law of nature, on another cause, by which it is determined in time.

In this sense freedom is a purely transcendental idea, which, first, contains nothing derived from *experience*, and, secondly, the object of which cannot be determined in any *experience*; because it is a general rule, even of the possibility of all *experience*, that everything which happens has a cause, and that therefore the causality also of the cause, which itself has happened or arisen, must again have a cause. In this manner the whole field of experience, however far it may extend, has been changed into one great whole of nature. As, however, it is impossible in this way to arrive at an absolute totality of the conditions in causal relations, reason creates for itself the idea of spontaneity, or the power of beginning by itself, without an antecedent cause determining it to action, according to the law of causal connection.

It is extremely remarkable, that the practical concept of freedom is founded on the *transcendental idea of freedom*, which constitutes indeed the real difficulty, which at all times has surrounded the question of the possibility of freedom. *Freedom*, in its *practical sense*, is the independence of our (arbitrary) will from the coercion through sensuous impulses. Our (arbitrary) will is *sensuous*, so far as it is *affected pathologically* (by sensuous impulses); it is called animal (*arbitrium brutum*), if necessitated pathologically. The human will is certainly sensuous, an *arbitrium sensitivum*, but not *brutum*, but *liberum*, because sensuous, impules do not necessitate its action, but there is in man a faculty of determination, independent of the necessitation through sensuous impulses.

It can easily be seen that, if all causality in the world of sense belonged to nature, every event would be determined in time through another, according to necessary laws. As therefore the phenomena, in determining the will, would render every act necessary as their natural effect, the annihilation of transcendental freedom would at the same time destroy all practical freedom. Practical freedom presupposes that, although something has not happened, it *ought* to have happened, and that its cause therefore had not that determining force among phenomena, which could prevent the causality of our will from producing, independently of those natural causes, and even contrary to their force and influence, something determined in the order of time, according to empirical laws, and from originating *entirely by itself* a series of events.

What happens here is what happens generally in the conflict of reason venturing beyond the limits of possible experience, namely, that the problem is not *physiological*, but *transcendental*. Hence the question of the possibility of freedom concerns no doubt psychology; but its solution, as it depends on dialectical arguments of pure reason, belongs entirely to transcendental philosophy. In order to enable that philosophy to give a satisfactory answer, which it cannot decline to do, I must first try to determine more accurately its proper procedure in this task.

If phenomena were things by themselves, and therefore space and time forms of the existence of things by themselves, the conditions together with the conditioned would always belong, as members, to one and the same series, and thus in our case also the antinomy which is common to all transcen-dental ideas would arise, namely, that that series is inevitably too large or too small for the understanding. The dynamical concepts of reason, however, which we have to discuss in this and the following section, have this peculiarity that, as they are not concerned with an object, considered as a quantity, but only with its *existence*, we need take no account of the quantity of the series of conditions. All depends here only on the dynamical relation of conditions to the conditioned, so that in the question on nature and freedom we at once meet with the difficulty, whether freedom is indeed possible, and whether, if it is possible, it can exist together with the universality of the natural law of causality. The question in fact arises, whether it is a proper disjunctive proposition to say, that every effect in the world must arise, *either* from nature, or from nature, *or* from freedom or whether *both* cannot co-exist in the same event in different relations. The correctness of the principle of the unbroken connection of all events in the world of sense, according to unchangeable natural laws, is firmly established by the transcendental Analytic, and admits of no limitation. The question, therefore, can only be whether, in spite of it, freedom also can be found in the same effect, which is determined by nature; or whether freedom is entirely excluded by that inviolable rule? Here the common but fallacious supposition of the *absolute reality* of phenomena shows at once its pernicious influence in embarrassing reason. For if phenomena are things by themselves, freedom cannot be saved. Nature in that case is the complete and sufficient cause determining every event, and its condition is always contained in that series of phenomena only which, together with their effect, are necessary under the law of nature. If, on the contrary, phenomena are taken for nothing except what they are in reality, namely, not things by themselves, but representations only, which are connected with each other according to empirical laws, they must themselves have causes, which are not phenomenal. Such an intelligible cause, however, is not determined with reference to its causality by phenomena, although its effects become phenomenal, and can thus be determined by other phenomena. That intelligible cause, therefore, with its causality, is outside the series, though its effect are to be found in the series of empirical conditions. The effect therefore can, with reference to its intelligible cause, be considered as free, and yet at the same time, with reference to phenomena, as resulting from them according to the necessity of nature; a distinction which, if thus represented, in a general and entirely abstract form, may seem extremely subtle and obscure, but will become clear in its practical application. Here I only wished to remark that, as the unbroken *connection* of all phenomena in the context (woof) of nature, is an unalterable law, it would necessarily destroy all freedom, if we were to defend obstinately the reality of phenomena. Those, therefore, who follow the common opinion on this subject, have never been able to reconcile nature and freedom.

Possibility of a causality through freedom, in harmony with the universal law of natural necessity

Whatever in an object of the senses is not itself phenomenal, I call *intelligible*. If, therefore, what in the world of sense must be considered as phenomenal, possesses in itself a faculty which is not the object of sensuous intuition, but through which it can become the cause of phenomena, the *causality* of that being may be considered from *two sides*, as *intelligible* in its *action*, as the causality of a thing by itself, and as *sensible* in the *effects* of the action, as the causality of a phenomenon in the world of sense. Of the faculty of such a being we should have to form both and *empirical* and an *intellectual concept* of its causality, both of which consist together in one and the same effect. This twofold way of conceiving the faculty of an object of the senses does not contradict any of the concepts, which we have to form of phenomena and of a possible experience. For as all phenomena, not being things by themselves, must have for their foundation a transcendental object, deter-mining them as mere representations, there is nothing to prevent us from attributing to that transcendental object, besides the quality through which it becomes phenomenal, a *causality* also which is not phenomenal, although its *effect* appears in the phenomenon. Every efficient cause, however, must have a *character*, that is, a rule according to which it manifests its causality, and without which it would not be a cause. According to this we should have in every subject of the world of sense, first, an *empirical character*, through which its acts, as phenomena, stand with other phenomena in an unbroken connection, according to permanent laws of nature, and could be derived from them as their conditions, and in connection with them form the links of one and the same series in the order of nature. Secondly, we should have to allow to it an *intelligible character* also, by which, it is true, it becomes the cause of the same acts as phenomena, but which itself is not subject to any conditions of sensibility, and never phenomenal. We might call the former the character of such a thing as a phenomenon, and the latter the character of the thing by itself.

According to its intelligible character, this active subject would not depend on conditions for time, for time is only the condition of phenomena, and not of things by themselves. In it no *act* would *arise* or *perish*, neither would it be subject therefore to the law of determination in time and of all that is changeable, namely, that everything *which happens* must have its cause in the *phenomena* (of the previous state). In one word its causality, so far as it is intelligible, would not have a place in the series of empirical conditions by which the event is rendered necessary in the world of sense. It is true that that intelligible character could never be known immediately, because we cannot perceive anything, except so far as it appears, but it would nevertheless have to be conceived, according to the empirical character, as we must always admit in thought a transcendental object, as the foundation of phenomena, though we know nothing of what it is by itself.

In its empirical character, therefore, that subject, as a phenomenon, would submit, according to all determining laws, to a causal nexus, and in that respect it would be nothing but a part of the world of sense, the effects of which, like every other phenomenon, would arise from nature without fail. As soon as external phenomena began to influence it, and as soon as its empirical character, that is the law of its causality, has been known through experience, all its actions ought to admit of explanation, according to the laws of nature, and all that is requisite for its complete and necessary determination would be found in a possible experience.

In its intelligible character, however (though we could only have a general concept of it), the same subject would have to be considered free from all influence of sensibility, and from all determination through phenomena: and as in it, so far as it is a *noumenon*, nothing *happens*, and no change which requires dynamical determination of time, and therefore no connection with phenomena as causes, can exist, that active being would so far be quite independent and free in its acts from all natural necessity, which can exist in the world sense only. One might say of it with perfect truth that it originates its effects in the world of sense *by itself*, though the act does not begin *in itself*. And this would be perfectly true, though the effects in the world of sense need not therefore originate by themselves, because in it they are always determined previously through empirical conditions in the previous time, though only by means of the empirical character (which is the phenomenal appearance of the intelligible character), and therefore impossible, except as a continuation of the series of natural causes. In this way freedom and nature, each in its complete signification, might exist together and without any conflict in the same action, according as we refer it to its intelligible or to its sensible cause.

Explanation of the cosmological idea of freedom in connection with the general necessity of nature

I thought it best to give first this sketch of the solution of our transcendental problem, so that the course which reason has to adopt in its solution might be more clearly surveyed. We shall now proceed to explain more fully the points on which the decision properly rest, and examine each by itself.

The law of nature, that everything which happens has a cause—that the causality of that is, its activity (as it is anterior in time, and, with regard to an effect which has *arisen*, cannot itself have always existed but must *happened* at some time), must have its cause among the phenomena by which it is determined, and that therefore all events in the order of nature are empirically determined, this law, I say, through which alone phenomena became *nature* and objects of experience, is a law of the understanding, which can on no account be surrendered, and from which no single phenomenon can be exempted; because in doing this we should place it outside all possible experience, separate from all objects of possible experience, and change it into a mere fiction of the mind or a cobweb of the brain.

But although this looks merely like a chain of causes, which in the regressus to its conditions admits of no *absolute totality*, this difficulty does not detain us in the least, because it has already been removed in the general criticism of the antinomy of reason when, starting from the series of phenomena, it aims at the unconditioned. Were we to yield to the illusion of transcendental realism, we should have neither nature nor freedom. The question therefore is, whether, if we recognize in the whole series of events nothing but natural necessity, we may yet regard the same event which on one side is an effect of nature only, on the other side, as an effect of freedom; or whether there is a direct contradiction between these two kinds of causality?

There can certainly be nothing among phenomenal causes that could originate a series absolutely and by itself. Every action, as a phenomenon, so far as its produces an event, is itself an event, presupposing another state, in which its cause can be discovered; and thus everything that happens is only a continuation of the series, and no beginning, happening by itself, is possible in it. Actions of natural causes in the succession of time are therefore themselves effects, which likewise presuppose causes in the series of time. A *spontaneous* and original action by which something takes place, which did not exist before, cannot be expected from the causal nexus of phenomena.

But is it really necessary that if effects are phenomena, the causality of their cause, which cause itself is phenomenal, could be nothing but empirical; or is it not possible, although for every phenomenal effect a connection with its cause, according to the laws of empirical causality, is certainly required, that empirical causality, itself could nevertheless, without breaking in the least its connection with the natural causes, represent an effect of a non-empirical and intelligible causality, that is, of a caused action, original in respect to phenomena, and in so far not phenomenal; but, with respect to this faculty, intelligible, although, as a link in the chain of nature, to be regarded as entirely belonging to the world of sense?

We require the principle of the causality of phenomena among themselves, in order to be able to look for and to produce natural conditions, that is, phenomenal causes of natural events. If this is admitted and not weakened by any exceptions, the under-standing, which in its empirical employment recognizes in all events nothing but nature, and is quite justified in doing so, has really all that it can demand, and the explanations of physical phenomena may proceed without let or hindrance. The understanding would not be wronged in the least, if we assumed, though it be a mere fiction, that some among the natural causes have a faculty which is intelligible only, and whose determination to activity does not rest on empirical conditions, but on mere grounds of the intellect, if only the *phenomenal activity* of that cause is in accordance with all the laws of empirical causality. For in this way the active subject, as *causa phaenomenon*, would be joined with nature through the indissoluble dependence of all its actions, and the phenomenon only of that subject (with all its phenomenal causality) would contain certain conditions which, if we want to ascend from the empirical to the transcendental object, would have to be considered as intelligible only. For, if only we follow the rule of nature in that which may be the cause among phenomena, it is indifferent to us what kind of ground of those phenomena, and of their connection, may be conceived to exist in the transcendental subject, which is empirically unknown to us. This intelligible ground does not touch the empirical questions, but concerns only, as it would seem, the thought in the pure understanding; and although the effects of that thought and action of the pure understanding may be discovered in the phenomena, these have nevertheless to be completely explained from their phenomenal cause, according to the laws of nature, by taking their empirical character as the highest ground of explanations, and passing by the intelligible character, which is the transcendental cause of the other, as entirely unknown, except so far as it is indicated by the empirical, as its sensuous sign. Let us apply this to experience. Man is one among the phenomena of the world of sense, and in so far one of the natural causes the causality of which must be subject to empirical laws. As such he must therefore have an empirical character, like all other objects of nature. We perceive it through the forces and faculties which he shows in his actions and effects. In the lifeless or merely animal nature we see no ground for admitting any faculty, except as sensuously conditioned. Man, however, who knows all the rest of nature through his senses only, knows himself through mere apperception also, and this in actions and internal determinations, which he cannot ascribe to the impressions of the senses. Man is thus to himself partly a phenomenon, partly, however, namely with reference to certain faculties, a purely intelligible object, because the actions of these faculties cannot be ascribed to the receptivity of sensibility. We call these faculties understanding and reason. It is the latter, in particular, which is entirely distinguished from all empirically conditioned forces or faculties, because it weights its objects according to ideas, and determines the understanding accordingly, which then makes an empirical use of its (by themselves, however pure) concepts.

That our reason possesses causality, or that we at least represent to ourselves such a causality in it, is clear from the *imperatives* which, in all practical matters, we impose as rules on our executive powers. The *ought* expresses a kind of necessity and connection with causes, which we do not find elsewhere in the whole of nature. The understanding can know in nature only what is present, past, or future. It is impossible that anything in it *ought to be* different from what it is in reality, in all these relations of time. Nay, if we only look at the course of nature, the ought has no meaning whatever. We cannot ask, what ought to be in nature, as little as we can ask, what qualities a circle ought to possess. We can only ask what happens in it, and what qualities that which happens has.

This *ought* expresses a possible action, the ground of which cannot be anything but a mere concept; while in every merely natural action the ground must always be a phenomenon. Now it is quite true that the action to which the ought applies must be possible under natural conditions, but these natural conditions do not affect the determination of the will itself, but only its effects and results among phenomena. There may be ever so many sensuous temptation, but they can never produce the *ought*, but only a willing which is always conditioned, but by not means necessary, and to which the ought, pronounced by reason, opposes measure, ay, prohibition and authority. Whether it be an object of the senses merely (pleasure), or of pure reason (the good), reason does not yield to the impulse that is given empirically, and does no follow the order of things, as they present themselves as phenomena, but frames for itself, with perfect spontaneity, a new order according to ideas to which it adapts the empirical conditions, and according to which it declares actions to be necessary, even though they *have not taken place*, and, maybe, never will take place. Yet it is presupposed that reason may have causality with respect to them, for otherwise no effects in experience could be expected to result from these ideas.

Now let us take our stand here and admit it at least as

possible, that reason really possesses causality with reference to phenomena. In that case, reason though it be, it must show nevertheless and empirical character, because every cause presupposes a rule according to which certain phenomena follow as effects, and every rule requires in the effects a homogeneousness, on which the concept of cause (as a faculty) is founded. This, so far as it is derived from mere phenomena, may be called the empirical character, which is *permanent*, while the effects, according to a diversity of concomitant, and in part, restraining conditions, appear in *changeable* forms.

Every man therefore has an empirical character of his (arbitrary) will, which is nothing but a certain causality of his reason, exhibiting in its phenomenal actions and effects a rule, according to which one may infer the motives of reason and its actions, both in kind and in degree, and judge of the subjective principles of his will. As that empirical character itself must be derived from phenomena, as an effect, and from their rule which is supplied by experience, all the acts of a man, so far as they are phenomena, are determined from his empirical character and from the other concomitant causes, according of the order of nature; and if we could investigate all the manifestations of his will to the very bottom, there would be not a single human action which we could not predict with certainty and recognize from its preceding conditions as necessary. There is no freedom therefore with reference to this empirical character, and yet it is only with reference to it that we can consider man, when we are merely *observing*, and, as is the case in anthropology, trying to investigate the motive causes of his actions physiologically.

If, however, we consider the same actions with reference to reason, not with reference to speculative reason, in order to *explain* their origin, but solely so far as reason is the cause which *produces* them; in one word, if we compare actions with reason, with reference to *practical* purposes, we find a rule and order, totally different from the order of nature. For, from this point of view, everything, it may be, *ought not to have happened*, which according to the course of nature *has happened*, and according to its empirical grounds, was inevitable. And sometimes we find, or believe at least that we find, that the ideas of reason have really proved their causality with reference to human actions as phenomena, and that these actions have taken place, not because they were determine by empirical causes, but by the causes of reason.

Now supposing one could say that reason possesses causality in reference to phenomena, could the action of reason be called free in that case, as it is accurately determined by the empirical character (the disposition) and rendered necessary by it? That character again is determined in the intelligible character (way of thinking). The latter, however, we do not know, but signify only through phenomena, which in reality give us immediately a knowledge of the disposition (empirical character) only.[12]

---

12. The true morality of actions (merit or guilt), even that of our own conduct, remains therefore entirely hidden. Our

An action, so far as it is to be attributed to the way of thinking as its cause, does nevertheless not result from it according to empirical laws, that is, it is not *preceded* by conditions of pure reason, but only by its effects in the phenomenal form of the internal sense. Pure reason, as a simple intelligible faculty, is not subject to the form of time, or to the conditions of the succession of time. The causality of reason in its intelligible character does *not arise* or begin at a certain time in order to produce an effect; for in that case it would be subject to the natural law of phenomena, which determines all causal series in time, and its causality would then be nature and not freedom. What, therefore, we can say is, that if reason can possess causality with reference to phenomena, it is a faculty *through which* the sensuous condition of an empirical series of effects first begins. For the condition that lies in reason is not sensuous, and therefore does itself not begin. Thus we get what we missed in all empirical series, namely, that the *condition* of a successive series of events should itself be empirically unconditioned. For here the condition is really *outside* the series of phenomena (in the intelligible), and therefore not subject to any sensuous condition, nor to any temporal determination through preceding causes.

---

imputations can refer to the empirical character only. How much of that may be the pure effect of freedom, how much should be ascribed to nature only, and to the faults of temperament, for which man is not responsible, or its happy constitution (*merito fortunae*), no one can discover, and no one can judge with perfect justice.

Nevertheless the same cause belongs also, in another respect, to the series of phenomena. Man himself is a phenomenon. His will has an empirical character, which is the (empirical) cause of all his actions. There is no condition, determining man according to this character, that is not contained in the series of natural effects and subject to their law, according to which there can be no empirically unconditioned causality of anything that happens in time. No given action therefore (as it can be perceived as a phenomenon only) can begin absolutely by itself. Of pure reason, however, we cannot say that the state in which it determines the will is preceded by another in which that state itself is determined. For as reason itself is not a phenomenon, and not subject to any of the conditions of sensibility, there exists in it, even in reference to its causality, no succession of time, and the dynamical law of nature, which determines the succession of time according to rules, cannot be applied to it.

Reason is therefore the constant condition of all free actions by which man takes his place in the phenomenal world. Every one of them is determined beforehand in his empirical character, before it becomes actual. With regard to the intelligible character, however, of which the empirical is only the sensuous schema, there is neither *before* nor *after*; and every action, without regard to the temporal relation which connects it with other phenomena, is the immediate effect of the intelligible character of pure reason. That reason therefore acts freely, without being determined dynamically, in the chain of natural causes, by external or internal condition, anterior in time. That freedom must then not only be regarded negatively, as independence of empirical conditions (for in that case the faculty of reason would cease to be a cause of phenomena), but should be determined positively also, as the faculty of beginning spontaneously a series of events. Hence nothing begins in reason itself, and being itself the unconditioned of every free action, reason admits of no condition antecedent in time above itself, while nevertheless its effect takes its beginning in the series of phenomena, though it can never constitute in that series an *absolutely* first beginning.

In order to illustrate the regulative principle of reason by an example of its empirical application, not in order to confirm it (for such arguments are useless for transcendental propositions), let us take a voluntary action, for example, a malicious lie, by which a man has produced a certain confusion in society, and of which we first try to find out the motives, and afterwards try to determine how far it and its consequences may by imputed to the offender. With regard to the first point, one has first to follow up his empirical character to its very sources, which are to be found in wrong education, bad society, in part also in the viciousness of a natural disposition, and a nature insensible to shame, or ascribed to frivolity and heedlessness, not omitting the occasioning causes at the time. In all this the procedure is exactly the same as in the investigation of a series of determining causes of a given natural effect. But although one believes that the act was thus determined, one nevertheless blames the offender, and not on account of his unhappy natural disposition, not on account of influencing circumstances, not even on account of his former course of life, because one supposes one might leave entirely out of account what that course of life may have been, and consider the past series of conditions as having never existed, and the act itself as totally unconditioned by previous states, as if the offender had begun with it a new series of effects, quite by himself. This blame is founded on a law of reason, reason being considered as a cause which, independent of all the before-mentioned empirical conditions, would and should have determined the behaviour of the man otherwise. Nay, we do not regard the causality of reason as a concurrent agency only, but as complete in itself, even though the sensuous motives did not favour, but even oppose it. The action is imputed to a man's intelligible character. At the moment when he tells the lie, the guilt is entirely his; that is, we regard reason, in spite of all empirical conditions of the act, as completely free, and the act has to be imputed entirely to a fault of reason.

Such an imputation clearly shows that we imagine that reason is not affected at all by the influences of the senses, and that it does not change (although its manifestations, that is the mode in which it shows itself by its effect, do change): that in it no state precedes as determining a following state, in fact, that reason does not belong to the series of sensuous conditions which render phenomena necessary, according to laws of nature. Reason, it is supposed, is present in all the actions of man, in all circumstances of time, and always the same; but it is itself never in time, never on a new state in which it was not before; it is *determining*, never *determined*. We cannot ask, therefore, why reason has not determined itself differently, but only why it has not differently determined the *phenomena* by its causality. And here no answer is really possible. For a different intelligible character would have given a different empirical character, and if we say that, in spite of the whole of his previous course of life, the offender could have avoided the lie, this only means that it was in the power of reason, and that reason, in its causality, is subject to no phenomenal and temporal conditions, and lastly, that the difference of time, though it makes a great difference in phenomena and their relation to each other, can, as these are neither things nor causes by themselves, produce no difference of action in reference to reason.

We thus see that, in judging of voluntary actions, we can, so far as the intelligible cause, but not beyond. We can see that that cause is free, that it determines as independent of sensibility, and therefore is capable of being the sensuously unconditioned condition of phenomena. To explain why that intelligible character should, under present circumstances, give these phenomena and this empirical character, and no other, transcends all the powers of our reason, nay, all its rights of questioning, as if we were to ask why the transcendental object of our external sensuous intuition gives us intuition in *space* only and no other. But the problem which we have to solve does not require us to ask or to answer such questions. Our problem was, whether freedom is contradictory to natural necessity in one and the same action: and this we have sufficiently answered by showing that freedom may have relation to a very different kind of conditions from those of nature, so that the law of the latter does not affect the former, and both may exist independent of, and undisturbed by, each other.

It should be clearly understood that, in what we have said, we had no intention of establishing the *reality* of freedom, as one of the faculties which contain the cause of the phenomenal appearances in our world of sense. For not only would this have been no transcendental consideration at all, which is concerned with concepts only, but it could never have succeeded, because from experience we can never infer anything but what must be represented in thought according to the law of experience. It was not even our intention to prove the *possibility* of freedom, for in this also we should not have succeeded, because from mere concepts *a priori* we can never know the possibility of any real ground or any causality. We have here treated freedom as a transcendental idea only, which makes reason imagine that it can absolutely begin the series of phenomenal conditions through what is sensuously unconditioned, but by which reason becomes involved in an antinomy with its own laws, which it had prescribed to the empirical use of the understanding. That this antinomy rests on a mere illusion, and that nature does *not contradict* the causality of freedom, that was the only thing which we could prove, and cared to prove.

Solution of the cosmological idea of the totality of the dependence of phenomena, with regard to their existence in general

In the preceding article we considered the changes in the world of sense in their dynamical succession, every one being subordinate to another as its cause. Now, however, the succession of states is to serve only as our guide in order to arrive at an existence that might be the highest condition of all that is subject to change, namely, the *necessary Being*. We are concerned here, not with the unconditioned existence of the substance itself. Therefore the succession which we have before us is properly one of concepts and not of intuitions, so far as the one is the condition of the other.

It is easy to see, however, that as everything comprehended under phenomena is changeable, and therefore conditioned in its existence, there cannot be, in the whole series of dependent existence, any unconditioned link, the existence of which might be considered as absolutely necessary, and that therefore, if phenomena were things by themselves, and their condition accordingly belonged with the conditioned always to one and the same series of intuitions, a necessary being, as the condition of the existence of the phenomena of the world of sense, could never exist.

The dynamical regressus has this peculiar distinction as compared with the mathematical, that, as the latter is only concerned with the composition of parts in forming a whole or the division of a whole into its parts, the conditions of that series must always be considered as part of it, and therefore as homogeneous and as phenomena, while in the dynamical regressus, where we are concerned, not with the possibility of an unconditioned part belonging to a given whole, but with the derivation of a state from its cause, or of the contingent existence of the substance itself from the necessary substance, it is not required that the condition should form one and the same empirical series with the conditioned.

There remains therefore to us another escape from this apparent antinomy; because both conflicting propositions might, under different aspects, be true at the same time. That is, all things of the world of sense might be entirely contingent, and have therefore an empirically conditioned existence only, though there might nevertheless be a non-empirical condition of the whole series, that is, an unconditionally necessary being. For this, as an intelligible condition, would not belong to the series, as a link of it (not even as the highest link), nor would it render any link of that series empirically unconditioned, but would leave the whole world of sense, in all its members, in its empirically conditioned existence. This manner of admitting an unconditioned existence as the ground of phenomena would differ from the empirically unconditioned causality (freedom) treated of in the preceding article, because, with respect to freedom, the thing itself, as cause (*substantia phaenomenon*), belonged to the series of conditions, and its causality only was represented as intelligible, while here, on the contrary, the necessary being has to be conceived as lying outside the series of the world of sense (as *ens extramundanum*), and as purely intelligible, by which alone it could be guarded against itself by becoming subject to the law of contingency and dependence applying to all phenomena.

The regulative principle of reason, with regard to our present problem, is therefore this, that everything in the world of sense has an empirically conditioned existence, and that in it there is never any unconditioned necessity with reference to any quality; that there is no member in the series of conditions of which one ought not to expect, and as far as possible to seek, the empirical condition in some possible experience; and that we are never justified in deriving any existence from a condition outside the empirical series, or in considering it as independent and self-subsistent in the series itself; without however denying in the least that that whole series may depend on some intelligible being, which is free therefore from all empirical conditions, and itself contains rather the ground of the possibility of all those phenomena.

By this we by no means intend to prove the unconditionally necessary existence of such a being, or even to demonstrate the possibility of a purely intelligible condition of the existence of the phenomena of the world of sense. But as on the one side we limit reason, least it should lose the thread of the empirical condition and lose itself in *transcendent* explanations incapable of being represented *in concreto*, thus, on the other side, we want to limit the law of the purely empirical use of the understanding, lest it should venture to decide on the possibility of things in general, and declare the intelligible to be *impossible*, because it has been shown to be useless for the explanation of phenomena. What is shown by this is simply this, that the complete contingency of all things in nature and of all the (empirical) conditions, may well coexist with the arbitrary presupposition of a necessary, though purely intelligible condition, and that, as there is no real contradiction between these two views, they *may well both be true*. Granted even that such an absolutely necessary being, as postulated by the understanding, is impossible in itself, we still maintain that this cannot be concluded from the general contingency and dependence of all that belongs to the world of sense, nor from the principle that we ought not to stop at any single member so far as it is contingent, and appeal to a cause outside the world. Reason follows its own course in its empirical, and again a peculiar course in its transcendental use.

The world of sense contains nothing but phenomena, and these are mere representations, which are always sensuously conditioned. As our objects are never things by themselves, we need not be surprised that we are never justified in making a jump from any member of the several empirical series, beyond the connection of sensibility, as if they were things by themselves, existing apart from their transcendental ground, and which we might leave behind in order to seek for the cause of their existence outside them. This, no doubt, would have to be done in the end with contingent *things*, but not with mere *representations* of things, the contingency of which is itself a phenomenon, and cannot lead to any other regressus but that which determines the phenomena, that is, which is empirical. To conceive, however, an intelligible ground of phenomena, that is, of the world of sense, and to conceive it as freed from the contingency of the latter, does not run counter either to the unlimited empirical regressus in the series of phenomena, nor to their general contingency. And this is really the only thing, which we had to do in order to remove this apparent antinomy, and which could be done in this wise only. For if every condition of everything conditioned (according to its existence) is sensuous, and therefore belongs to the series, that series is again conditioned (as shown in the antithesis of the fourth antinomy). Either therefore there would remain a conflict with reason, which postulates the unconditioned, or this would have to be placed outside the series, *i.e.* in the intelligible, the necessity of which neither requires nor admits of any empirical condition, and is therefore, as regards phenomena, unconditionally necessary.

The empirical use of reason (with regard to the conditions of existence in the world of sense) is not affected by the admission of a purely intelligible being, but ascends, according to the principle of general contingency, form empirical conditions to higher ones, which again are empirical. This regulative principle, however, does not exclude the admission of an intelligible cause not comprehended in the series, when we come to the pure use of reason (with reference to ends or aims). For in this case, an intelligible cause only means the transcendental, and, to us, unknown ground of the possibility of the sensuous series in general, and the existence of this, independent of all conditions of the sensuous series, and, in reference to it, unconditionally, necessary, is by no means opposed to the unlimited contingency of the former, nor to the never-ending regressus in the series of empirical conditions.

Concluding remark on the whole antimony of pure reason

So long as it is only the totality of the conditions in the world of sense and the interest it can have to reason, that form the object of the concepts of our reason, our ideas are no doubt transcendental, but yet *cosmological*. If, however, we place the unconditioned (with which we are chiefly concerned) in that which is entirely outside the world of sense, therefore beyond all possible experience, our ideas become *transcendent*: for they serve not only for the completion of the empirical use of the understanding (which always remains an idea that must be obeyed, though it can never be fully carried out), but they separate themselves entirely from it, and create to themselves objects the material of which is not taken from experience, and the objective reality of which does not rest on the completion of the empirical series, but on pure concepts *a priori*. Such transcendent ideas have a merely intelligible object, which may indeed be admitted as transcendental object, of which, for the rest, we know nothing, but for which, if we wish to conceive it as a thing determined by its internal distinguishing predicates, we have neither grounds of possibility (as indepent of all concepts of experience) nor the slightest justification on our side in admitting it as an object, and which, therefore, is a mere creation of our thoughts. Nevertheless that cosmological idea, which owes its origin to the fourth antinomy, urges us on to take that step. For the conditioned existence of all phenomena, not being founded in itself, requires us to look out for something different from all phenomena, that is, for an intelligible objects in which there should be no more contingency. As, however, if we have once allowed ourselves to admit, outside the field of the whole of sensibility, a reality existing by itself, phenomena can only be considered as contingent modes of representing intelligible objects on the part of beings which themselves are intelligences, nothing remains to us, in order to form some kind of concept of intelligible things, of which in themselves we have not the slightest knowledge, but analogy, applied to the concepts of experience. As we know the contingent by experience only, but have here to deal with things which are not meant to be objects of experience, we shall have to derive our knowledge of them from what is necessary in itself, that is from pure concepts of things in general. Thus the first step which we take outside the world of sense, obliges us to begin our new knowledge with the investigation of the absolutely necessary Being, and to derive from its concepts the concepts of all things, so far as they are intelligible only.

Fundamental Principles of the Metaphysic of Morals

The autonomy of the will as the supreme principles of morality

Autonomy of the will is that property of it by which it is law to itself (independently on any property of the objects of volition). The principle of autonomy then is: Always so to choose that the same volition shall comprehend the maxims of our choice as a universal law. We cannot prove that this practical rule is an imperative, *i.e.* that the will of every rational being is necessarily bound to it as a condition, by a mere analysis of the conceptions which occur in it, since it is a synthetical proposition; we must advance beyond the cognition of the objects to a critical examination of the subject, that is of the pure practical reason, for this synthetic proposition which commands apodictically must be capable of being cognized wholly *a priori*. This matter, however, does not belong to the present section. But that the principle of autonomy in question is the sole principle of morals can be readily shown by mere analysis of the conception of morality. For by this analysis we find that its principle must be a categorical imperative, and that what this commands is neither more nor less than this very autonomy.

Heteronomy of the will as the source of all spurious principles of morality

If the will seeks the law which is to determine it *anywhere else* than in the fitness of its maxims to be universal laws of its own dictation, consequently if it goes out of itself and seeks this law in the character of any of its objects, there always results *heteronomy*. The will in that case does not give itself the law, but it is given by the object through its relation to the will. This relation, whether it rests on inclination or on any conceptions of reason, only admits of hypothetical imperatives: I ought to do something *because I wish for something else*. On the contrary, the moral, and therefore categorical, imperative says: I ought to do so and so, even though I should not wish for anything else. *Ex. gr.*, the former says: I ought not to lie if I would retain my reputation; the latter says: I ought not to lie although it should not bring me the least discredit. The latter therefore must so far abstract from all objects that they shall have no *influence* on the will, in order that practical reason (will) may not be restricted to administering an interest not belonging to it, but may simply show its own commanding authority as the supreme legislation. Thus, ex. gr., I ought to endeavour to promote the happiness of others, not as if its realization involved any concern of mine (whether by immediate inclination or by any satisfaction indirectly gained through reason), but simply because a maxim which excludes it cannot be comprehended as a universal law in one and the same volition.

Of all principles of morality which can be founded on the conception of heteronomy

Here as elsewhere human reason in its pure use, so long as it was not critically examined, has first tied all possible wrong ways before it succeeded in finding the one true way.

All principles which can be taken from this point of view are either *empirical* or *rational*. The *former*, drawn from the principle of happiness, are built on physical or moral feelings; the *latter*, drawn from the principle of *perfection*, are built either on the rational conception of perfection as a possible effect, or on that of an independent perfection (the will of God) as the determining cause of our will.

Empirical principle are wholly incapable of serving as a foundation for moral laws. For the universality with which these should hold for all rational beings without distinction, the unconditional practical necessity, which is thereby impossed on them is lost when their foundation is taken from the *particular constitution of human nature*, or the accidental circumstances in which it is placed. The principle of *private happiness*, however, is the most objectionable, not merely because it is false, and experience contradicts the supposition that prosperity is always proportioned to good conduct, nor yet merely because it contributes nothing to the establishment of morality—since it is quite a different thing to make a prosperous man and a good man, or to make one prudent and sharp-sighted for his own interests, and to make him virtuous—but because the springs it provides for morality are such as rather undermine it and destroy its sublimity, since they put the motives to virtue and to vice in the same class, and only teach us to make a better calculation, the specific difference between virtue and vice being entirely extinguished. On the other hand, as to moral feeling, this supposed special sense, the appeal to it is indeed superficial when those who cannot *think* believe that *feeling* will help them out, even in what concerns general laws: and besides, feelings which naturally differ infinitely in degree cannot furnish a uniform standard of good and evil, nor has anyone a right to form judgments for others by his own feelings: nevertheless this moral feeling is nearer to morality and its dignity in this respect, that it pays virtue the honour of ascribing to her *immediately* the satisfaction and esteem we have for her, and does not, as it were, tell her to her face that we are not attracted to her by her beauty but by profit.

Critique of Practical Reason

Preface

This work is called the "Critical examination of Practical Reason," not of the *pure* practical reason although its parallelism with the speculative critique, would seem to require the latter term. The reason of this appears sufficiently from the treatise itself. Its business is to show that there is *pure practical reason*, and for this purpose it criticizes the entire practical *faculty* of reason. If it succeeds in this, it has no need to criticize the *pure faculty itself* in order to see whether reason in making such a claim does not presumptuously *overstep* itself (as is the case with the speculative reason). For if, as pure reason, it is actually practical, it proves its own reality and that of its concepts by fact, and all disputation against the possibility of its being real is futile.

With this faculty, transcendental freedom is also established; freedom, namely, in that absolute sense in which speculative reason required it in its use of the concept of causality in order to escape the antinomy into which it inevitably falls, when in the chain of cause and effect it tries to think the *unconditioned*. Speculative reason could only exhibit this concept (of freedom) problematically as not impossible to thought, without assuring it any objective reality, and merely lest the supposed impossibility of what it must at least allow to be thinkable should endanger its every being and plunge it into an abyss of scepticism.

Inasmuch as the reality of the concept of freedom is proved by an apodictic law of practical reason, it is the *keystone* of the whole system of pure reason, even the speculative, and all other concepts (those of God and immortality) which, as being mere ideas, remain in it unsupported, now attach themselves to this concept, and by it obtain consistence and objective reality; that is to say, their *possibility* is *proved* by the fact that freedom actually exists, for this is revealed by the moral law.

Freedom, however, is the only one of all the ideas of the speculative reason of law which we *know* the possibility *a priori* (without, however, understanding it), because it is the condition of the moral law which we know. The ideas of *God* and *Immortality*, however, are not conditions of the moral law, but only conditions of the necessary object of a will determined by this law: that is to say, conditions of the practical use of our pure reason. Hence with respect to these ideas we cannot affirm that we *know* and *understand*, I will not say the actuality, but even the possibility of them. However, they are the conditions of the application of the morally determined will to its object, which is given to it *a priori*, viz., the *summum bonum*. Consequently in this practical point of view their possibility must be *assumed*, although we cannot theoretically know and understand it. To justify this assumption it is sufficient, in a practical point of view, that they contain no intrinsic impossibility (contradiction). Here we have what, as far as speculative reason is concerned, is a merely *subjective* principle of assent, which, however, is objectively valid for a reason equally pure but practical, and this principle, by means of the concept of freedom assures objective reality and authority to the ideas of God and Immortality. Nay, there is a subjective necessity (a need of pure reason) to assume them. Nevertheless the theoretical knowledge of reason is not hereby enlarged, but only the possibility is given, which heretofore was merely a *problem*, and now becomes *assertion*, and thus the practical use of reason is connected with the elements of theoretical reason. And this need is not a merely hypothetical one for the arbitrary purposes of speculation, that we must assume something if we *wish* in speculation to carry reason to its utmost limits, but it is a need which has the force of *law* to assume something without which that cannot be which we must inevitably set before us as the aim of our action.

Fundamental law of the pure practical reason

Act so that the maxim of thy will can always at the same time hold good as a principle of universal legislation.

Remark

Pure geometry has postulates which are practical propositions, but contain nothing further than the assumption that we *can* do something if it is required that we *should* do it, and these are only geometrical propositions that concern actual existence. They are, then, practical rules under a problematical condition of the will: but here the rule says:—We absolutely must proceed in a certain manner. The practical rule is, therefore unconditional, and hence it is conceived *a priori* as a categorically practical proposition by which the will is objectively determined absolutely and immediately (by the practical rule itself, which thus is in this case a law); for *pure reason practical of itself* is here directly legislative. The will is thought as independent on empirical conditions, and, therefore, as pure will determined by *the mere form of the law*, and this principle of determination is regarded as the supreme condition of all maxims. The thing is strange enough, and has no parallel in all the rest of our practical knowledge. For the *a priori* thought of a possible universal legislation which is therefore merely problematical, is unconditionally commanded as a law without borrowing anything from experience or from any external will. This, however, is not a precept to do something by which some desired effect can be attained (for then the will would depend on physical conditions), but a rule that determines the will *a priori* only so far as regards the forms of its maxims; and thus it is at least not impossible to conceive that a law, which only applies to the *subjective* form of principles, yet serves as a principle of determination by means of the *objective* form of law in general. We may call the consciousness of this fundamental law a mere fact of reason, because we cannot reason it out from antecedent data of reason, *e.g.* the consciousness of freedom (for this is not antecedently given), but it forces itself on us as a synthetic *a priori* proposition, which is not based on any intuition, either pure or empirical. It would, indeed, be analytical if the freedom of the will were presupposed, but to presuppose freedom as a positive *concept* would require an intellectual intuition, which cannot here be assumed; however, when we regard the law as *given*, it must be observed, in order not to fall into any misconception, that it is not an empirical fact, but the sole fact of the pure reason which thereby announces itself as originally legislative (*sic volo sic jubeo*).

Corollary

Pure reason is practical of itself alone, and gives (to man) a universal law which we call the *Moral Law*.

Remark

The fact just mentioned is undeniable. It is only necessary to analyse the judgment that men pass on the lawfulness of their actions, in order to find that, whatever inclination may say to the contrary, reason, incorruptible and self-constrained, always confronts the maxim of the will in any action with the pure will, that is, with itself, considering itself as *a priori* practical. Now this principle of morality, just on account of the universality of the legislation which makes it the formal supreme determining principle of the will, without regard to any subjective differences, is declared by the reason to be a law for all rational beings, in so far as they have a will, that is, a power to determine their causality by the conception of rules; and, therefore, so far as they are capable of acting according to principles, and consequently also according to practical *a priori* principles (for these alone have the necessity that reason requires in a principle). It is, therefore, not limited to men only, but applies to all finite beings that posses reason and will; nay, it even includes the Infinite Being as the supreme intelligence. In the former case, however, the law has the form of an imperative, because in them, as rational beings, we can suppose a *pure* will, but being creatures affected with wants and physical motives, not a *holy* will, that is, one which would be incapable of any maxim conflicting with the moral law. In their case, therefore, the moral law is an *imperative* which commands categorically, because the law is unconditioned; the relation of such a will to this law is *dependence* under the name of *obligation*, which implies a *constraint* to an action, though only by reason and its objective law; and this action is called duty, because an elective will, subject to pathological affections (though not determined by them, and therefore still free), imples a wish that arises from *subjective* causes, and therefore may often be opposed to the pure objective determining principle; whence it requires the moral constraint of a resistance of the practical reason, which may be called an internal, but intellectual, compulsion. In the supreme intelligence the electric will is rightly conceived as incapable of any maxim which could not at the same time be objectively a law; and the notion of a *holiness*, which on that account belongs to it, places it, not indeed above all practical laws, but above all practically restrictive laws, and consequently above obligation and duty. This holiness of will is, however, a practical idea, which must necessarily serve as a type to which finite rational beings can only approximate indefinitely, and which the pure moral law which is itself on this account called holy, constantly and rightly holds before their eyes. The utmost that finite practically reason can effect is to be certain of this indefinite progress of one's maxims, and of their steady disposition to advance. This is virtue, and virtue, at least as a naturally acquired faculty, can never be perfect, because assurance in such a case never becomes apodictic certainty, and when it only amounts to persuasion is very dangerous.

Of the motives of pure practical reason

What is essential in the moral worth of actions is *that the moral law should directly determine the will*. If the determination of the will takes place in conformity indeed to the moral law, but only by means of a feeling, no matter of what kind, which has to be presupposed in order that the law may be sufficient to determine the will, and therefore not *for the sake of the law*, then the action will possess legality but not morality. Now, if we understand by *motive* (or *spring*) (*elater animi*) the subjective ground of determination of the will of a being whose reason does not necessarily conform to the objective law, by virtue of its own nature, then it will follow, first, that no motives can be attributed to the Divine will, and that the motives of the human will (as well as that of every created rational being) can never be anything else than the moral law, and consequently that the objective principle of determination must always and alone be also the subjectively sufficient determining principle of the action, if this is not merely to fulfil the *letter* of the law, without containing its *spirit*.

Since, then, for the purpose of giving the moral law influence over the will, we must not seek for any other motives that might enable us to dispense with the motive of the law itself, because that would produce mere hypocrisy, without consistency; and it is even *dangerous* to allow other motives (for instance, that of interest) even to co-operate along with the moral law; hence nothing is left us but to determine carefully in what way the moral law becomes a motive, and what effect this has upon the faculty of desire. For as to the question how a law can be directly and of itself a determining principle of the will (which is the essence of morality), this is, for human reason, an insoluble problem and identical with the question: how a free will is possible. Therefore what we have to show *a priori* is, not why the moral law in itself supplies a motive, but what effect it, as such, produces (or, more correctly speaking, must produce) on the mind.

The essential point in every determination of the will by the moral law, is that being a free will it is determined simply by the moral law, not only without the co-operation of sensible impulses, but even to the rejection of all such, and to the checking of all inclinations so far as they might be opposed to that law. So far, then, the effect of the moral law as a motive is only negative, and this motive can be known *a priori* to be such. For all inclination and every sensible impulse is founded on feeling, and the negative effect produced on feeling (by the check on the inclinations) is itself feeling; consequently, we can see *a priori* that the moral law, as a determining principle of the will, must by thwarting all our inclinations produce a feeling which may be called pain; and in this we have the first, perhaps the only, instance in which we are able from *a priori* considerations to determine the relation of a cognition (in this case of pure practical reason) to the feeling of pleasure or displeasure. All the inclinations together (which can be reduced to a tolerable system, in which case their satisfaction is called happiness) constitute *self-regard* (*solopsismus*). This is either the *self-love* that consists in an excessive *fondness* for oneself (*philautia*), or satisfaction with oneself (*arrogantia*). The former is called particularly *selfishness*; the latter *self-conceit*. Pure practical reason only *checks* selfishness, looking on it as natural and active in us even prior to the moral law, so far as to limit it to the condition of agreement with this law, and then it is called *rational self-love*. But self-conceit reason strikes *down* altogether, since all claims to self-esteem which precede agreement with the moral law are vain and unjustifiable, for the certainty of a state of mind that coincides with this law is the first condition of personal worth (as we shall presently show more clearly), and prior to this conformity any pretension to worth is false and unlawful. Now the propensity to self-esteem is one of the inclinations which the moral law checks, inasmuch as that esteem rests only on morality. Therefore the moral law breaks down self-conceit. But as this law is something positive in itself, namely, the form of an intellectual causality, that is of freedom, it must be an object of respect; for by opposing the subjective antagonism of the inclinations it *weakens* self-conceit; and since it even *breaks down*, that is, humiliates this conceit, it is an object of the highest respect, and consequently is the foundation of a positive feeling which is not of empirical origin, but is known *a priori*. Therefore respect for the moral law is a feeling which is produced by an intellectual cause, and this feeling is the only one that we know quite *a priori*, and the necessity of which we can perceive.

In the preceding chapter we have seen that everything that presents itself as an object of the will prior to the moral law is by that law itself, which is the supreme condition of practical reason, excluded from the determining principles of the will which we have called the unconditionally good; and that the mere practical form which consists in the adaptation of the maxims to universal legislation first determines what is good in itself and absolutely, and is the basis of the maxims of a pure will, which alone is good in every respect. However, we find that our nature as sensible beings is such that the matter of desire (objects of inclination, whether of hope or fear) first presents itself to us; and our pathologically affected self, although it is in its maxims quite unfit for universal legislation, yet, just as if it constituted our entire self, strives to put its pretensions forward first, and to have them acknowledged as the first and original. This propensity to make ourselves in the subjective determining principles of our choice serves as the objective determining principle of the will generally may be called self-love; and if this pretends to be legislative as an unconditional principle, it may be called *self-conceit*. Now the moral law, which alone is truly objective (namely, in every respect), entirely excludes the influence of self-love on the supreme practical principle, and indefinitely checks the self-conceit that prescribes the subjective conditions of the former as laws. Now whatever checks our self-conceit in our own judgment humiliates; therefore the moral law inevitably humbles every man when he compares with it the physical propensities of his nature. That, the idea of which as a *determining principle of our will* humbles us in our self-consciousness, awakes *respect* for itself, so far as it is itself positive, and a determining principle. Therefore the moral law is even subjectively a cause of respect. Now since everything that enters into self-love belongs to inclination, and all inclination rests on feelings, and consequently whatever checks all the feelings together in self-love has necessarily, by this very circumstance, an influence on feeling; hence we comprehend how it is possible to perceive *a priori* that the moral can produce an effect on feeling, in that it excludes the inclinations and the propensity to make them the supreme practical condition *i.e.* self-love, from all participation in the supreme legislation. This effect is on the one side merely *negative*, but on the other side, relatively to the restricting principle of pure practical reason, it is *positive*. No special kind of feeling need be assumed for this under the name of a practical or moral feeling as antecedent to the moral law, and serving as its foundation.

The negative effect on feeling (unpleasantness) is *pathological*, like every influence on feeling, and like every feeling generally. But as an effect of the consciousness of the moral law, and consequently in relation to a supersensible cause, namely, the subject of pure practical reason which is the supreme lawgiver, this feeling of a rational being affected by inclinations is called humiliation (intellectual self-depreciation); but with reference to the positive source of this humiliation, the law, it is respect for it. There is indeed no feeling for this law; but inasmuch as it removes the resistance out of the way, this removal of an obstacle is, in the judgment of reason, esteemed equivalent to a positive help to its causality. Therefore, this feeling may also be called a feeling of respect for the moral law, and for both reasons together *a moral feelings*.

While the moral law, therefore, is a formal determining principle of action by practical pure reason, and is moreover a material though only objective determining principle of the objects of action as called good and evil, it is also a subjective determining principle, that is, a motive to this action, inasmuch as it has influence on the morality of the subject, and produces a feeling conducive to the influence of the law on the will. There is here in the subject no *antecedent* feeling tending to morality. For this is impossible, since every feeling is sensible, and the motive of moral intention must be free from all sensible conditions. On the contrary, while the sensible feeling which is at the bottom of all our inclinations is the condition of that impression which we call respect, the cause that determines it lies in the pure practical reason; and this impression therefore, on account of its origin, must be called, not a pathological but a *practical effect*. For by the fact that the conception of the moral law deprives self-love of its influence, and self-conceit of its illusion, it lessens the obstacle to pure practical reason, and produces the conception of the superiority of its objective law to the impulses of the sensibility; and thus, by removing the counterpoise, it gives relatively greater weight to the law in the judgment of reason (in the case of a will affected by the aforesaid impulses). Thus the respect for the law is not a motive to morality, but is morality itself subjectively considered as a motive, inasmuch as pure practical reason, by rejecting all the rival pretensions of self-love, gives authority to the law, which now alone has influence. Now it is to be observed that as respect is an effect on feeling, and therefore on the sensibility, of a rational being, it presupposes this sensibility, and therefore also the finiteness of such beings on whom the moral law imposes respect; and that respect for the *law* cannot be attributed to a supreme being, or to any being free from all sensibility, in whom, therofore, this sensibility cannot be an obstacle to practical reason.

This feeling (sentiment) (which we call the moral feeling) is therefore produced simply by reason. It does not serve for the estimation of actions nor for the foundation of the objective moral law itself, but merely as a motive to make this of itself a maxim. But what name could we more suitably apply to this singular feeling which cannot be compared to any pathological feeling? It is of such a peculiar kind that it seems to be at the disposal of reason only, and that pure practical reason.

Respect applies always to persons only—not to things. The latter may arouse inclination, and if they are animals (*e.g.* horses, dogs, etc.), even *love* or *fear*, like the sea, a volcano, a beast of prey; but never *respect*. Something that comes nearer to this feeling is *admiration*, and this, as an affection, astonishment, can apply to things also, *e.g.* lofty mountains, the magnitude, number, and distance of the heavenly bodies, the strength and swiftness of many animals, etc. But all this is not respect. A man also may be an object to me of love, fear, or admiration, even to astonishment, and yet not be an object of respect. His jocose humour, his courage and strength, his power from the rank he has amongst others, may inspire me with sentiments of this kind, but still inner respect for him is wanting. *Fontenelle* says, "I bow before a great man, but my mind does not bow." I would add, before an humble plain man, in whom I perceive uprightness of character in a higher degree than I am conscious of in myself, *my mind bows* whether I choose it or not, and though I bear my head never so high that he may not forget my superior rank. Why is this? Because his example exhibits to me a law that humbles my self-conceit when I compare it with my conduct: a law, the *practicability* of obedience to which I see proved by fact before my eyes. Now, I may even be conscious of a like degree of uprightness, and yet the respect remains. For since in man all good is defective, the law made visible by an example still humbles my pride, my standard being furnished by a man whose imperfections, whatever they may be, are not known to me as my own are, and who therefore appears to me in a more favourable light. *Respect* is a *tribute* which we cannot refuse to merit, whether we will or not; we may indeed outwardly withhold it, but we cannot help feeling it inwardly.

Respect is so *far from being* a feeling of pleasure that we only reluctantly give way to it as regards a man. We try to find out something that may lighten the burden of it, some fault to compensate us for the humiliation which such an example causes. Even the dead are not always secure from this criticism, especially if their example appears inimitable. Even the moral law itself in its *solemn majesty* is exposed to this endeavour to save oneself from yielding it respect. Can it be thought that it is for any other reason that we are so ready to reduce it to the level of our familiar inclination, or that it is for any other reason that we all take such trouble to make it out to be the chosen precept of our own interest well understood, but that we want to be free from the deterrent respect which shows us our own unworthiness with such severity? Nevertheless, on the other hand, so *little* is there *pain* in it that if once one has laid aside self-conceit and allowed practical influence to that respect, he can never be satisfied with contemplating the majesty of this law, and the soul believes itself elevated in proportion as it sees the holy law elevated above it and its frail nature. No doubt great talents and activity proportioned to them may also occasion respect for an analogous feeling. It is very proper to yield it to them, and then it appears as if this sentiment were the same thing as admiration. But if we look closer, we shall observe that it is always uncertain how much of the ability is due to native talent, and how much to diligence in cultivating it. Reason represents it to us as probably the fruit of cultivation, and therefore as meritorious, and this notably reduces our self-conceit, and either casts a reproach on us or urges us to follow such an example in the way that is suitable to us. This respect, then, which we show to such a person (properly speaking, to the law that his example exhibits) is not mere admiration; and this is confirmed also by the fact, that when the common run of admirers think they have learned from any source the badness of such a man's character (for instance, Voltaire's), they give up all respect for him; whereas the true scholar still feels it at least with regard to his talents, because he is himself engaged in a business and a vocation which makes imitation of such a man in some degree a law.

Respect for the moral law is therefore the only and the undoubted moral motive, and this feeling is directed to no object, except on ground of this law. The moral law first determines the will objectively and directly in the judgment of reason; and freedom, whose causality can be determined only by the law, consists just in this, that it restricts all inclinations, and consequently self-esteem, by the condition of obedience to its pure law. This restriction now has an effect on feeling, and produces the impression of displeasure which can be known *a priori* from the moral law. Since it is so far only a *negative* effect which, arising from the influence of pure practical reason, checks the activity of the subject, so far as it is determined by inclinations, and hence checks the opinion of his personal worth (which, in the absence of agreement with the moral law, is reduced to nothing); hence, the effect of this law on feeling is merely humiliation. We can, therefore, perceive this *a priori*, but cannot know by it the force of the pure practical law as a motive, but only the resistance of the sensibility. But since the same law is objectively, that is, in the conception of pure reason, an immediate principle of determination of the will, and consequently this humiliation takes place only relatively to the purity of the law; hence, the lowering of the pretensions of moral self-esteem, that is, humiliation on the sensible side, is an elevation of the moral, *i.e.* practical, esteem for the law itself on the intellectual side; in a word, it is respect for the law, and therefore, as its cause is intellectual, a positive feeling which can be known *a priori*. For whatever diminishes the obstacles to an activity furthers this activity itself. Now the recognition of the moral law is the consciousness of an activity of practical reason from objective principles, which only fails to reveal its effect in actions because subjective (pathological) causes hinder it. Respect for the moral law, then, must be regarded as a positive, though indirect, effect of it on feeling, inasmuch as this respect weakens the impeding influence of inclinations by humiliating self-esteem; and hence also as a subjective principle of activity, that is, as a *motive* to obedience to the law, and as a principle of the maxims of a life conformable to it. From the notion of a motive arises that of an *interest*, which can never be attributed to any being unless it possesses reason, and which signifies a *motive* of the will in so far as it is conceived by the reason. Since in a morally good will the law itself must be the motive, the *moral interest* is a pure interest of practical reason alone, independent on sense. On the notion of an interest is based that of a *maxim*. This, therefore, is morally good only in case it rests simply on the interest taken in obedience to the law. All three notions, however, that of a *motive*, of an *interest*, and of a *maxim*, can be applied only to finite beings. For they all suppose a limitation of the nature of the being, in that the subjective character of his choice does not of itself agree with the objective law of a practical reason; they suppose that the being requires to be impelled to action by something, because an internal obstacle opposes itself. Therefore they cannot be applied to the Divine will.

There is something so singular in the unbounded esteem for the pure moral law, apart from all advantage, as it is presented for our obedience by practical reason, the voice of which makes even the boldest sinner tremble, and compels him to hide himself from it, that we cannot wonder if we find this influence of a mere intellectual idea on the feelings quite incomprehensible to speculative reason, and have to be satisfied with seeing so much of this *a priori*, that such a feeling is inseparably connected with the conception of the moral law in every finite rational being. If this feeling of respect were pathological, and therefore were a feeling of pleasure based on the inner *sense*, it would be in vain to try to discover a connection of it with any idea *a priori*. But (it) is a feeling that applies merely to what is practical, and depends on the conception of a law, simply as to its form, not on account of any object, and therefore cannot be reckoned either as pleasure or pain, and yet produces an *interest* in obedience to the law, which we call the *moral interest*, just as the capacity of taking such an interest in the law (or respect for the moral law itself) is properly the *moral feeling* (or *sentiment*).

The consciousness of a *free* submission of the will to the law, yet combined with an inevitable constraint put upon all inclinations, though only by our own reason, it respect for the law. The law that demands this respect and inspires it is clearly no other than the moral (for no other precludes all inclinations from exercising any direct influence on the will). An action which is objectively practical according to this law, to the exclusion of every determining principle of inclination, is *duty*, and this by reason of that exclusion includes in its concept practical *obligation*, that is, a determination to actions, however *reluctantly* they may be done. The feeling that arises from the consciousness of this obligation is not pathological, as would be a feeling produced by an object of the senses but practical only, that is, it is made possible by a preceding (objective) determination of the will and causality of the reason. As *submission* to the law, therefore, that is, as a command (announcing constraint for the sensibly affected subject), it contains in it no pleasure, but on the contrary, so far, pain in the action. On the other hand, however, as this constraint is exercised merely by the legislation of our *own* reason, it also contains something elevating, and this subjective effect on feeling, inasmuch as pure practical reason is the sole cause of it, may be called in this respect self-*approbation*, since we recognize ourselves as determined thereto solely by the law without any interest, and are now conscious of a quite different interest subjectively produced thereby, and which is purely practical and *free*; and our taking this interest in an action of duty is not suggested by any inclination, but is commanded and actually brought about by reason through the practical law; whence this feeling obtains special name, that of respect.

The notion of duty, therefore, requires in the action, *objectively*, agreement with the law, and, subjectively in its maxim, that respect for the law shall be the sole mode in which the will is determined thereby. And on this rests the distinction between the consciousness of having acted *according to duty* and *from duty*, that is, form respect for the law. The former (*legality*) is possible even if inclinations have been the determining principles of the will; but the latter (*morality*), moral worth, can be placed only in this, that the action is done from duty, that is, simply for the sake of the law.

It is of the greatest importance to attend with the utmost exactness in all moral judgements to the subjective principle of all maxims, that all the morality of actions may be placed in the necessity of acting *from duty* and from respect for the law, not from love and inclination for that which the actions are to produce. For men and all created rational beings moral necessity is constraint, that is obligation, and every action based on it is to be conceived as a duty, not as a proceeding previously pleasing, or likely to be pleasing to us of our own accord. As if indeed we could ever bring it about that without respect for the law, which implies fear, or at least apprehension of transgression, we of ourselves, like the independent Deity, could ever come into possession of *holiness* of will by the coincidence of our will with the pure moral law becoming as it were part of our nature, never to be shaken (in which case the law would cease to be a command for us, as we could never be tempted to be untrue to it).

The moral law is in fact for the will of a perfect being a law of *holiness*, but for the will of every finite rational being a law of *duty*, of moral constraint, and of the determination of its actions by *respect* for this law and reverence for its duty. No other subjective principle must be assumed as a motive, else while the action might chance to be such as the law prescribes, yet as it does not proceed from duty, the intention, which is the thing properly in question in this legislation, is not moral.

It is a very beautiful thing to do good to men from love to them and from sympathetic good will, or to be just from love of order; but his is not yet the true moral maxim of our conduct which is suitable to our position amongst rational beings as *men*, when we pretend with fanciful pride to set ourselves above the though of duty, like volunteers, and, as if we were independent on the command, to want to do of our own good pleasure what we think we need no command to do. We stand under a *discipline* of reason, and in all our maxims must not forget our subjection to it, nor withdraw anything therefrom, or by an egotistic presumption diminish aught of the authority of the law (although our own reason gives it) so as to set the determining principle of our will, even though the law be conformed to, anywhere else but in the law itself and in respect for this law. Duty and obligation are the only names that we must give to our relation to the moral law. We are indeed legislative members of a moral kingdom rendered possible by freedom, and presented to us by reason as an object of respect; but yet we are subjects in it, not the sovereign, and to mistake our inferior position as creatures, and presumptuously to reject the authority of the moral law, is already to revolt from it in spirit, even though the letter of it is fulfilled.

With this agrees very well the possibility of such a command as: *Love God above everything, and thy neighbour as thyself*. For as a command it requires respect for a law which *commands* love and does not leave it to our own arbitrary choice to make this our principle. Love to God, however, considered as an inclination (pathological love), is impossible, for He is not an object of the senses. The same affection towards men is possible no doubt, but cannot be commanded, for it is not in the power of any man to love anyone at command; therefore it is only *practical love* that is meant in that pith of all laws.

To love God means, in this sense, to like to do His commandments; to love one's neighbour means to like to practise all duties towards him. But the command that makes this a rule cannot command us to *have* this disposition in actions conformed to duty, but only to *endeavour* after it. For a command to like to do a thing is in itself contradictory, because if we already know of ourselves what we are bound to do, and if further we are conscious of liking to do it, a command would be quite needless; and if we do it not willingly, but only out of respect for the law, a command that makes this respect the motive of our maxim would directly counteract the disposition commanded. That law of all laws, therefore, like all the moral precepts of the Gospel, exhibits the moral disposition in all its perfection, in which, viewed as an ideal of holiness, it is not attainable by any creature, but yet is the pattern which we should strive to approach, and in an uninterrupted but infinite progress become like to. In fact, if a rational creature could ever reach this point, that he thoroughly likes to do all moral laws, this would mean that there does not exist in him even the possibility of a desire that would tempt him to deviate from them; for to overcome such a desire always costs the subject some sacrifice, and therefore requries self-compulsion, that is, inward constraint to something that one does not quite like to do; and no creature can ever reach this stage of moral disposition. For, being a creature, and therefore always dependent with respect to what he requires for complete satisfaction, he can never be quite free from desires and inclinations, and as these rest on physical causes, they can never of themselves coincide with the moral law, the sources of which are quite different; and therefore they makes it necessary to found the mental disposition of one's maxims on moral obligation, not on ready inclination, but on respect, which *demands* obedience to the law, even though one may not like it; not on love, which apprehends no inward reluctance of the will towards the law. Nevertheless, this latter, namely, love to the law (which would then cease to be a command, and then morality, which would have passed subjectively into holiness, would cease to be *virtue*), must be the constant though unattainable goal of his endeavours. For in the case of what we highly esteem, but yet (on account of the consciousness of our weakness) dread, the increased facility of satisfying it changes the most reverential awe into inclination, and respect into love; at least this would be the perfection of a disposition devoted to the law, if it were possible for a creature to attain it.

This reflection is intended not so much to clear up the evangelical command just cited, in order to prevent *religious fanaticism* in regard to love of God, but to define accurately the moral disposition with regard directly to our duties towards men, and to check, or if possible prevent, *a merely moral fanaticism* which infects many persons. The stage of morality on which man (and, as far as we can see, every rational creature) stands is respect for the moral law. The disposition that he ought to have in obeying this is to obey it from duty, not from spontaneous inclination, or from an endeavour taken up from liking and unbidden; and this proper moral condition in which he can always be is *virtue*, that is, moral disposition *militant*, and not *holiness* in the fancied *possession* of a perfect *purity* of the disposition of the will. It is nothing but moral fanaticism and exaggerated self-conceit that is infused into the mind by exhortation to actions as noble, sublime, and magnanimous, by which men are led into the delusion that it is not duty, that is, respect for the law, whose yoke (an easy yoke indeed, because reason itself imposes it on us) they *must* bear, whether they like it or not, that constitutes the determining principle of their actions, and which always humbles them while they *obey* it; fancying that those actions are expected from them, not from duty, but as pure merit. For not only would they, in imitating such deeds from such a principle, not have fulfilled the spirit of the law in the least, which consists not in the legality of the action (without regard to principle), but in the subjection of the mind to the law; not only do they make the motives *pathological* (seated in sympathy or self-love), not moral (in the law), but they produce in this way a vain, high-flying, fantastic way of thinking, flattering themselves with a spontaneous goodness of heart that needs neither spur nor bridle, for which no command is needed, and thereby forgetting their obligation, which they ought to think of rather than merit. Indeed actions of others which are done with great sacrifice, and merely for the sake of duty, may be praised as *noble* and *sublime*, but only so far as there are traces which suggest that they were done wholly out of respect for duty and not from excited feelings. If these, however, are set before anyone as examples to be imitated, respect for duty (which is the only true moral feeling) must be employed as the motive—this severe holy precept which never allows our vain self-love to dally with pathological impulses (however analogous they may be to morality), and to take a pride in *meritorious* worth. Now if we search we shall find for all actions that are worthy of praise a law of duty which *commands*, and does not leave us to choose what may be agreeable to our inclinations. This is the only way of representing things that can give a moral training to the soul, because it alone is capable of solid and accurately defined principles.

If *fanaticism* in its most general sense is a deliberate overstepping of the limits of human reason, then *moral fanaticism* is such an overstepping of the bounds that practical pure reason sets to mankind, in that it forbids us to place the subjective determining principle of correct actions, that is, their moral motive, in anything but the law itself, or to place the disposition which is thereby brought into the maxims in anything but respect for this law, and hence commands us to take as the supreme *vital principal* of all morality in men the thought of duty, which strikes down all *arrogance* as well as vain *self-love*.

If this is so, it is not only writers of romance or sentimental educators (although they may be zealous opponents of sentimentalism), but sometimes even philosopher, nay, even the severest of all, the Stoics, that have brought in *moral fanaticism* instead of a sober but wise moral discipline, although the fanaticism of the latter was more heroic, that of the former of an insipid, effeminate character; and we may, without hypocrisy, say of the moral teaching of the Gospel, that it first, by the purity of its moral principle, and at the same time by its suitability to the limitations of finite beings, brought all the good conduct of men under the discipline of a duty plainly set before their eyes, which does not permit them to indulge in dreams of imaginary moral perfections; and that it also set the bounds of humility (that is, self-knowledge) to self-conceit as well as to self-love, both which are ready to mistake their limits.

Duty! Thou sublime and mighty name that dost embrace nothing charming or insinuating, but requirest submission, and yet seekest not to move the will by threatening aught that would arouse natural aversion or terror, but merely holdest forth a law which of itself finds entrance into the mind, and yet gains reluctant reverence (though not always obedience), a law before which all inclinations are dumb, even though they secretly coutnerwork it; what origin is there worthy of thee, and where is to be found the root of thy noble descent which proudly rejects all kindred with the inclinations; a root to derived from which is the indispensable condition of the only worth which men can give themselves?

It can be nothing less than a power which elevates man above himself (as a part of the world of sense), a power which connects him with an order of things that only the understanding can conceive, with a world which at the same time commands the whole sensible world, and with it the empirical determinable existence of man in time, as well as the sum-total of all ends (which totality alone suits such unconditional practical laws as the moral). This power is nothing but personality, that is, freedom and independence on the mechanism of nature, yet, regarded also as a faculty of a being which is subject to special laws, namely, pure practical laws given by its own reason; so that the person as belonging to the sensible world is subject to his own personality as belonging to the intelligible (supersensible) world. It is, then, not to be wondered at that man, as belonging to both worlds, must regard his own nature in reference to its second and highest characteristic only with reverence, and its laws with the highest respect.

On this origin are founded many expressions which designate the worth of objects according to moral ideas. The moral law is *holy* (inviolable). Man is indeed unholy enough; but he must regard *humanity* in his own person as holy. In all creation everything one chooses, and over which one has any power, may be used *merely as means*; man alone, and with him every rational creature, is an *end in himself*. By virtue of the autonomy of his freedom he is the subject of the moral law, which is holy. Just for this reason every will, even every person's own individual will, in relation to itself, is restricted to the condition of agreement with the *autonomy* of the rational being, that is to say, that it is not to be subject to any purpose which cannot accord with a law which might arise from the will of the passive subject himself; the latter is, therefore, never to be employed merely as means but as itself also, concurrently, an end. We justly attribute this condition even to the Divine will, with regard to the rational beings in the world, which are His creatures, since it rests on their *personality*, by which alone they are ends in themselves.

This respect-inspiring idea of personality which sets before our eyes the sublimity of our nature (in its higher aspect), while at the same time it shows us the want of accord of our conduct with it, and thereby strikes down self-conceit, is even natural to the commonest reason, and easily observed. Has not every even moderately honourable man sometimes found that, where by an otherwise inoffensive lie he might either have withdrawn himself from an unpleasant business, or even have procured some advantage for a loved and well-deserving friend, he has avoided it solely lest he should despise himself secretly in his own eyes? When an upright man is in the greatest distress, which he might have avoided if he could only have disregarded duty, is he not sustained by the consciousness that he has maintained humanity in its proper dignity in his own person and honoured it, that he has no reason to be ashamed of himself in his own sight, or to dread the inward glance of self-examination? This consolation is not happiness it is not even the smallest part of it, for no one would wish to have occasion for it, or would perhaps even desire a life in such circumstances. But he lives, and he cannot endure that he should be in his own eyes unworthy of life. This inward peace is therefore merely negative as regards what can make life pleasant; it is, in fact, only the escaping the danger of sinking in personal worth, after everything else that is valuable has been lost. It is the effect of a respect of something quite different from life, something in comparison and contrast with which life with all its enjoyment has no value. He still lives only because it is his duty, not because he finds anything pleasant in life.

Such is the nature of the true motive of pure practical reason; it is no other than the pure moral law itself, inasmuch as it makes us conscious of the sublimity of our own supersensible existence, and subjectively produces respect for their higher nature in men who are also concious of their pathologically very susceptible nature. Now with this motive may be combined so many charms and satisfactions of life, that even on this account alone the most prudent choice of a rational *Epicurean* reflecting on the greatest advantage of life would declare itself on the side of moral conduct, and it may even be advisable to join this prospect of a cheerful enjoyment of life with that supreme motive which is already sufficient of itself; but only as a counterpoise to the attractions which vice does not fail to exhibit on the opposite side, and not so as, even in the smallest degree, to place in this the proper moving power when duty is in question. For that would be just the same as to wish to taint the purity of the moral disposition in its source. The majesty of duty has nothing to do with eniovment of life: it has its special law and its special tribunal, and though the two should be never so well shaken together to be given well mixed, like medicine, to the sick soul, yet they will soon separate of themselves; and if they do not, the former will not act; and although physical life might gain somewhat in force, the moral life would fade away irrecoverably.

Critical examination of the analytic of pure practical reason

By the critical examination of a science, or of a portion of it, which constitutes a system by itself, I understand the enquiry and proof why it must have this and no other systematic form, when we compare it with another system which is based on a similar faculty of knowledge. Now practical and speculative reason are based on the same faculty, so far as both are *pure reason*. Therefore the difference in their systematic form must be assigned.

The Analytic of pure theoretic reason had to do with the knowledge of such objects as may have been given to the understanding, and was obliged therefore to begin from *intuition*, and consequently (as this is always sensible) from sensibility; and only after that could advance to concepts (of the objects of this intuition), and could only end with *principle* after both these had preceded. On the contrary, since practical reason has not to do with objects so as to *know* them, but with its own faculty of *realizing* them (in accordance with the knowledge of them), that is, with a will which is a causality, inasmuch as reason contains its determining principle; since consequently it has not to furnish an object of intuition, but as practical reason has to furnish only a law (because the notion of causality always implies the reference to a law which determines the existence of the many in relation to one another); hence a critical examination of the Analytic of reason, if this is to be practical reason (and this is properly the problem), must begin with the *possibility of practical principles a priori*. Only after that can it proceed to *concepts* of the objects of a practical reason, namely, those of absolute good and evil, in order to assign them in accordance with those principles (for prior to those principles they cannot possibly be given as good and evil by any faculty of knowledge), and only then could the section be concluded with the last chapter, that namely, which treats of the relation of the pure practical reason to the sensibility and of its necessary influence thereon, which is a *priori* cognizable, that is, of the *moral sentiment*. Thus the Analytic of the practical pure reason has the whole extent of the conditions of its use in common with the theoretical, but in reverse order. The Analytic of pure theoretic reason was divided into transcendental Aesthetic and transcendental Logic, that of the practical reversely into Logic and Aesthetic of pure practical reason (if I may, for the sake of analogy merely, use these designations, which are not quite suitable). This logic again was there divided into the Analytic of concepts and that of principles: here into that of principles and concepts. The Aesthetic also had in the former cases two parts, on account of the two kinds of sensible intuition; here the sensibility is not considered as a capacity of intuition at all, but merely as feeling (which can be a subjective ground of desire), and in regard to it pure practical reason admits no further division.

It is also easy to see the reason why this division into two parts with its subdivision was not actually adopted here (as one might have been induced to attempt by the example of the former critique). For since it is *pure reason* that is here considered in its practical use, and consequently as proceeding from *a priori* principles, and not from empirical principles of determination, hence the division of the analytic of pure practical reason must resemble that of a syllogism, namely, proceeding from the universal in the *major premiss* (the moral principle), through a *minor premiss* containing a subsumption of possible actions (as good or evil) under the former, to the *conclusion*, namely, the subjective determination of the will (an interest in the possible practical good, and in the maxim founded on it). He who has been able to convince himself of the truth of the positions occurring in the Analytic will take pleasure in such comparisons; or they justly suggest the expectation that we may perhaps some day be able to discern the unity of the whole faculty of reason (theoretical as well as practical), and be able to derive all from one principle, which is what human reason inevitably demands, as it finds complete satisfaction only in a perfectly systematic unity of its knowledge.

If now we consider also the contents of the knowledge that we can have of a pure practical reason, and by means of it, as shown by the Analytic, we find, along with a remarkable analogy between it and the theoretical, no less remarkable differences. As regards the theoretical, the *faculty of a pure rational cognition a priori* could be easily and evidently proved by examples from sciences (in which, as they put their principles to the test in so many ways by methodical use, there is not so much reason as in common knowledge to fear a secret mixture of empirical principles of cognition). But, that pure reason without the admixture of any empirical principle is practical of itself, this could only be shown from the *commonest practical use of reason*, by verifying the fact, that every man's natural reason acknowledges the supreme practical principle as the supreme law of his will—a law completely *a priori*, and not depending on any sensible data. It was necessary first to establish and verify the purity of its origin, even in the *judgment of this common reason*, before science could take it in hand to make use of it, as a fact, that is, prior to all disputation about its possibility, and all the consequences that may be drawn from it. but this circumstance may be readily explained from what has just been said; because practical pure reason must necessarily begin with principles, which therefore must be the first data, the foundation of all science, and cannot be derived from it. It was possible to effect the verification of moral principles as principles of a pure reason quite well, and with sufficient certainty, by a single appeal to the judgement of common sense, for this reason, that anything empirical which might slip into our maxims as a determining principle of the will can be detected at once by the feeling of pleasure or pain which necessarily attaches to it as exciting desire; whereas pure practical reason positively *refuses* to admit this feeling into its principle as a condition. The heterogeneity of the determining principles (the empirical and rational) is clearly detected by this resistance of a practically legislating reason against every admixture of inclination, and by a peculiar kind of sentiment, which, however, does not precede the legislation of the practical reason, but, on the contrary, is produced by this as a constraint, namely, by the feeling of a respect such as no man has for inclinations of whatever kind but for the law only; and it is detected in so marked and prominent a manner that even the most uninstructed cannot fail to see at once in an example presented to him, that empirical principles of volition may indeed urge him to follow their attractions, but that he can never be expected to *obey* anything but the pure pracitcal law of reason alone.

The distinction between the *doctrine of happiness* and the *doctrine of morality* (*ethics*), in the former of which empirical principles constitute the entire foundation, while in the second they do not form the smallest part of it, is the first and most important office of the analytic of pure practical reason; and it must proceed in it with as much *exactness* and, so to speak, *scrupulousness* as any geometer in his work. The philosopher, however, has greater difficulties to contend with here (as always in rational cognition by means of concepts merely without construction), because he cannot take any intuition as a foundation (for a pure noumenon). He has, however, this advantage that, like the chemist, he can at any time make an experiment with every man's practical reason for the purpose of distinguishing the moral (pure) principle of determination from the empirical, namely, by adding the moral law (as a determining principle) to the empirically affected will (*e.g.* that of the man who would be ready to lie because he can gain something thereby). It is as if the analyst added alkali to a solution of lime in hydrochloric acid, the acid at once forsakes the lime, combines with the alkali, and the lime is precipitated. Just in the same way, if to a man who is otherwise honest (or who for this occasion places himself only in thought in the position of an honest man), we present the moral law by which he recognizes the worthlessness of the liar, his practical reason (informing a judgement of what ought to be done) at once forsakes the advantage, combines with that which maintains in him respect for his own person (truthfulness), and the advantage after it has been separated and wasted from every particle of reason (which is altogether on the side of duty) is easily weighed by everyone, so that it can enter into combination with reason in other cases, only not where it could be opposed to the moral law, which reason never forsakes, but most closely unites itself with.

But it does not follow that this distinction between the principle of happiness and that of morality is an *opposition* between them, and pure practical reason does not require that we should *renounce* all claim to happiness but only that the moment duty is in question we should take *no account* of happiness. It may even in certain respects be a duty to provide for happiness; partly, because (including skill, wealth, riches) it contains means for the fulfilment of our duty; partly, because the absence of it (*e.g.* poverty) implies temptation to transgress our duty. But it can never be an immediate duty to promote our happiness, still less can it be the principle of all duty. Now, as all determining principle of the will, except the law of pure practical reason alone (the moral law) are all empirical, and therefore, as such belong to the principle of happiness, they must all be kept apart from the supreme principle of morality, and never be incorporated with it as a condition; since this would be to destroy all moral worth just as much as any empirical admixture with geometrical principles would destroy the certainty of mathematical evidence, which in Plato's opinion is the most excellent thing in mathematics, even surpassing their utility.

Instead, however, of the deduction of the supreme principle of pure practical reason, that is, the explanation of the possibility of such a knowledge *a priori*, the utmost we were able to do was to show that if we saw the possibility of the freedom of an efficient cause, we should also see not merely the possibility, but even the necessity of the moral law as the supreme practical law of rational beings, to whom we attribute freedom of causality of their will; because both concepts are so inseparably united, that we might define pracitcal freedom as independence of the will on anything but the moral law. But we cannot perceive the possibility of the freedom of an efficient cause, especially in the world of sense; we are fortunate if only we can be sufficiently assured that there is no proof of its imposibility, and are now by the moral law which postulates it compelled, and therefore authorized to assume it. However, there are still many who think that they can explain this freedom on empirical principles, like any other physical faculty, and treat it as a *psychological* property, the explanation of which only requires a more exact study of the *nature of the soul* and of the motives of the will, and not as a *transcendental* predicate of the causality of a being that belongs to the world of sense (which is really the point). They thus deprive us of the grand revelation which we obtain through practical reason by means of the moral law, the revelation, namely, of a supersensible world by the realization of the otherwise transcendent concept of freedom, and by this deprive us also of the moral law itself, which admits no empirical principle of determination. Therefore it will be necessary to add something here as a protection against this delusion, and to exhibit *empiricism* in its naked superficiality.

The notion of causality as *physical necessity*, in opposition to the same notion as *freedom*, concerns only the existence of things so far as it is *determinable in time*, and, consequently, as phenomena, in opposition to their causality as things in themselves. Now if we take the attributes of existence of things in time for attributes of things in themselves (which is the common view), then it is impossible to reconcile the necessity of the causal relation with freedom; they are contradictory. For from the former it follows that every event, and consequently every action that takes place at a certain point of time, is a necessary result of what existed in time preceding. Now as time past is no longer in my power, hence every action that I perform must be the necessary result of certain determining grounds *which are not in my power*, that is, at the moment in which I am acting I am never free. Nay, even if I assume that my whole existence is independent on any foreign cause (for instance, God), so that the determining principles of my causality, and even of my whole existence, were not outside myself, yet this would not in the least transform that physical necessity into freedom. For at every moment of time I am still under the necessity of being determined to action by that which is *not in my power*, and the series of events infinite *a parte priori* which I only continue according to a pre-determined order, and could never begin of myself, would be a continuous physical chain, and therefore my causality would never be freedom.

If, then, we would attribute freedom to a being whose existence is determined in time, we cannot except him from the law of necessity as to all events in his existence, and consequently as to his actions also; for that would be to hand him over to blind chance. Now as this law inevitably applies to all the causality of things, so far as their *existence* is determinable *in time*, it follows that if this were the mode in which we had also to conceive the *existence of these things in themselves*, freedom must be rejected as a vain and impossible conception. Consequently, if we would still save it, no other way remains but to consider that the existence of a thing, so far as it is determinable in time, and therefore its causality, according to the law of physical necessity, belong to *appearance*, and to attribute *freedom to the same being as a thing in itself*. This is certainly inevitable, if we would retain both these contradictory concepts together; but in application when we try to explain their combination in one and the same action, great difficulties present themselves which seem to render such a combination impracticable.

When I say of a man who commits a theft that, by the

physical law of causality, this deed is a necessary result of the determining causes in preceding time, then it was impossible that it could not have happened; how then can the judgment, according to the moral law, make any changes, and suppose that it could have been omitted, because the law says that it ought to have been omitted: that is, how can a man be called quite free at the same moment, and with respect to the same action in which he is subject to an inevitable physical necessity? Some try to evade this by saying that the causes that determine his causality are of such a *kind* as to agree with *comparative* notion of freedom. According to this, that is sometimes called a free effect, the determining physical cause of which lies *within* in the acting thing itself, *e.g.* that which a projectile performs when it is in free motion, in which case we use the word "freedom," because while it is in flight it is not urged by anything external; or as we call the motion of a clock free motion, because it moves its hands itself, which therefore do not require to be pushed by external force, so although the actions of man are necessarily determined by causes which precede in time, we yet call them free, because these causes are ideas produced by our own faculties, whereby desires are evoked on occasion of circumstances, and hence actions are wrought according to our own pleasure. This is a wretched subterfuge with which some person still let themselves be put off, and so think they have solved, with a petty word-jugglery, that difficult problem, at the solution of which centuries have laboured in vain, and which can therefore scarcely be found so completely on the surface. In fact, in the question about the freedom which must be the foundation of all moral laws and the consequent responsibility, it does not matter whether the principles which necessarily determine causality by a physical law reside *within* the subject or *without* him, or in the former case whether these principle are instinctive or are conceived by reason, if as is admitted by these men themselves, these determining ideas have the ground of their existence in time and in the *antecedent state*, and this again in an antecedent, etc. then it matters not that these are internal; it matters not that they have a psychological and not a mechanical causality, that is, produce actions by means of ideas, and not by bodily movements; they are still *determining principles* of the causality of a being whose existence is determinable in time, and therefore under the necessitation of conditions of past time, which therefore, when the subject has to act, are *no longer in his power*. This may imply psychological freedom (if we choose to apply this term to a merely internal chain of ideas in the mind), but it involves physical necessity, and therefore leaves no room for *transcendental freedom* which must be conceived as independence on everything empirical, and, consequently, on nature generally, whether it be an object of the internal sense considered in time only, or of the external in time and space. Without this freedom (in the latter and true sense), which alone is practical *a priori*, no moral law and no moral imputation are possible. Just for this reason the necessity of events in time, according to the physical law of causality, may be called the *mechanism* of nature, although we do not mean by this that things which are subject to it must be really material *machines*. We look here only to the necessity of the connection of event in a time-series as it is developed according to the physical law, whether the subject in which this development takes place is called *automation materiale* when the mechanical being is moved by matter, or with Leibnitz *spirituale* when it is impelled by ideas; and if the freedom of our will were no other than the latter (say the psychological and comparative, not also transcendental, that is, absolute), then it would at bottom be noting better than the freedom of a turnspit, which, when once it is wound up, accomplishes its motions of itself.

Now in order to remove in the supposed case the apparent contradiction between freedom and the mechanism of nature in one and the same action, we must remember what was said in the *Critique of Pure Reason*, or what follows therefrom, viz. that the necessity of nature, which cannot co-exist with the freedom of the subject, appertains only to the attributes of the thing that is subject to time-conditions, consequently only to those of the acting subject as a phenomenon; that therefore in this respect the determining principles of every action of the same reside in what belongs to past time, and is *no longer in his power* (in which must be included his own past actions and the character that these may determine for him in his own eyes as a phenomenon). But the very same subject being on the other side conscious of himself as a thing in himself, considers his existence also in *so far as it is not subject to time-conditions*, and regards himself as only determinable by laws which he gives himself through reason; and in this his existence nothing is antecedent to the determination of his will, but every action, and in general every modification of his existence, varying according to his internal sense, even the whole series of his existence as a sensible being, is in the consciousness of his super-sensible existence nothing but the result, and never to be regarded as the determining principle of his causality as a *noumenon*. In this view now the rational being can justly say of every unlawful action that he performs, that he could very well have left it undone; although as appearance it is sufficiently determined in the past, and in this respect is absolutely necessary; for it, with all the past which determines it, belongs to the one single phenomenon of his character which he makes for himself, in consequence of which he imputes the causality of those appearances to himself as a cause independent on sensibility.

With this agree perfectly the judicial sentences of that wonderful faculty in us which we call conscience. A man may use as much art as he likes in order to paint to himself an unlawful act that he remembers, as an unintentional error, a mere oversight, such as one can never altogether avoid, and therefore as something in which he was carried away by the stream of physical necessity, and thus to make himself out innocent, yet he finds that the advocate who speaks in his favour can by no means silence the accuser within, if only he is conscious that at the time when he did this wrong he was in his senses, that is, in possession of his freedom; and, nevertheless, he accounts for his error from some bad habits, which by gradual neglect of attention he has allowed to grow upon him to such a degree that he can regard his error as its natural consequence, although this cannot protect him from the blame and reproach which he casts upon himself. This is also the ground of repentance for a long past action at every recollection of it; a painful feeling produced by the moral sentiment, and which is practically void in so far as it cannot serve to undo what has been done. (Hence *Priestley*, as a true and consistent *fatalist*, declares it absurd, and he deserves to be commended for this candour more than those who, while they maintain the mechanism of the will in fact, and its freedom in words only, yet wish it to be thought that they include it in their system of compromise, although they do not explain the possibility of such moral imputation.) But the pain is quite legitimate, because when the law of our intelligible (supersensible) existence (the moral law) is in question, reason recognizes no distinction of time, and only asks whether the event belongs to me, as my act, and then always morally connects the same feeling with it, whether it has happened just now or long ago. For in reference to the *supersensible* consciousness of its existence (*i.e.* freedom) the *life of sense* is but a single phenomenon, which, inasmuch as it contains merely manifestations of the mental disposition with regard to the moral law (*i.e.* of the character), must be judged not according to the physical necessity that belongs to it as phenomenon, but according to the absolute spontaneity of freedom. It may therefore be admitted that if it were possible to have so profound an insight into a man's mental character as shown by internal as well as external actions, as to know all its motives, even the smallest, and likewise all the external occasions that can influence them, we could calculate a man's conduct for the future with as great certainty as a lunar or solar eclipse; and nevertheless we may maintain that the man is free. In fact, if we were capable of a further glance, namely, an intellectual intuition of the same subject (which indeed is not granted to us, and instead of it we have only the rational concept), then we should perceive that this whole chain of appearances in regard to all that concerns the moral laws depends on the spontaneity of the subject as a thing in itself, of the determination of which no physical explanation can be given. In default of this intuition the moral law assures us of this distinction between the relation of our actions as appearance to our sensible nature, and the relation of this sensible nature to the supersensible substratum in us. In this view, which is natural to our reason, though inexplicable, we can also justify some judgments which we passed with all conscientiousness, and which yet at first sight seem quite opposed to all equity. There are cases in which men, even with the same education which has been profitable to others, yet show such early depravity, and so continue to progress in it to years of manhood, that they are thought to be born villains, and their character altogether incapable of improvement; and nevertheless they are judged for what they do or leave undone, they are reproached for their faults as guilty; nay, they themselves (the children) regard these reproaches as well founded, exactly as if in spite of the hopeless natural quality of mind ascribed to them, they remained just as responsible as any other man. This could not happen if we did not suppose that whatever springs from a man's choice (as every action intentionally performed undoubtedly does) has as its foundation a free causality, which from early youth expresses its character in its manifestations (*i.e.* actions). These, on account of the uniformity of conduct, exhibit a natural connection, which, however, does not make the vicious quality of the will necessary, but, on the contrary, is the consequence of the evil principles voluntarily adopted and unchangeable, which only make it so much the more culpable and deserving of punishment. There still remains a difficulty in the combination of freedom with the mechanism of nature in a being belonging to the world of sense: a difficulty which, ever after all the foregoing is admitted, threatens freedom with complete destruction. But with this danger there is also a circumstance that offers hope of an issue still favourable to freedom, namely, that the same difficulty presses much more strongly (in fact, as we shall presently see, presses only) on the system that holds the existence determinable in time and space to be the existence of things in themselves; it does not therefore oblige us to give up our capital supposition of the ideality of time as a mere form of sensible intuition, and consequently as a mere manner of representation which is proper to the subject as belonging to the world of sense; and therefore it only requires that this view be reconciled with this idea (of freedom).

The difficulty is as follows:—Even if it is admitted that the supersensible subject can be free with respect to a given action, although as a subject also belonging to the world of sense, he is under mechanical conditions with respect to the same action; still, as soon as we allow that *God* as universal first cause is also *the cause of the existence of substance* (a proposition which can never be given up without at the same time giving up the notion of God as the Being of all beings, and therewith giving up His all-sufficiency, on which everything in theology depends), it seems as if we must admit that a man's actions have their determining principle in something *which is wholly out of his power*, namely, in the causality of a Supreme Being distinct from himself, and on whom his own existence and the whole determination of his causality are absolutely dependent. In point of fact, if a man's actions as belonging to his modifications in time were not merely modification of him as appearance, but as a thing in itself, freedom could not be saved. Man would be a marionette or an automaton, like Vaucanson's prepared and wound up by the Supreme Artist. Self-consciousness would indeed make him a thinking automaton; but the consciousness of his own spontaneity would be mere delusion if this were mistaken for freedom, and it would deserve this name only in comparative sense, since, although the proximate determining causes of its motion and a long series of the determining causes are internal, yet the last and highest is found in a foreign land. Therefore I do not see how those who still insist on regarding time and space as attributes belonging to the existence of things in themselves, can avoid admitting the fatality of actions; or if (like the otherwise acute Mendelssohn) they allow them to be conditions necessarily belonging to the existence of finite and derived beings, but not to that of the infinite supreme Being, I do not see on what ground they can justify such a distinction, or, indeed, how they can avoid the contradiction that meets them, when they hold that existence in time is an attribute necessarily belonging to finite things in themselves, whereas God is the cause of this existence, but cannot be the cause of time (or space) itself (since this must [on this hypothesis] be presupposed as a necessary *a priori* condition of the existence of things); and consequently as regards the existence of these things His causality must be subject to conditions, and even to the condition of time; and this would inevitably bring in everything contradictory to the notions of His infinity and independence. One the other hand, it is quite easy for us to draw the distinction between the attribute of the divine existence of being independent on all time-conditions, and that of a being of the world of sense, the distinction being that between the *existence of a being in itself* and that of a *thing in appearance*. Hence, if this ideality of time and space is not adopted, noting remains but *Spinozism*, in which space and time are essential attributes of the Supreme Being Himself, and the things dependent on Him (ourselves, therefore, included) are not substances, but merely accidents inhering in Him; since, if these things as His effects exist *in time* only, this being the condition of their existence in themselves, then the actions of these beings must be simply His actions which He performs in some place and time. Thus Spinozism, in spite of the absurdity of its fundamental idea, argues more consistently than the creation theory can, when beings assumed to be substances, and beings in themselves *existing in time*, are regarded as effects of a Supreme Cause, and yet as not belonging to Him and His action, but as separate substances.

The above-mentioned difficulty is resolved briefly and clearly as follows:—If existence *in time* is a mere sensible mode of representation belonging to thinking beings in the world, and consequently does not apply to them as things in themselves, then the creation of these beings is a creation of things in themselves, since the notion of creation does not belong to the sensible form of representation of existence or to causality, but can only be referred to noumena. Consequently, when I say of beings in the world of sense that they are created, I so far regard them as noumena. As it would be a contradiction, therefore, to say that God is a creator of appearances, so also it is a contradiction to say that as creator He is the cause of actions in the world of sense, and therefore as appearances, although He is the cause of the existence of the acting beings (which are noumena). If now it is possible to affirm freedom in spite of the natural mechanism of actions as appearances (by regarding existence in time as something that belongs only to appearances, not to things in themselves), then the circumstance that the acting beings are creatures cannot make the slightest difference, since creation concerns their supersensible and not their sensible existence, and therefore cannot be regarded as the determining principle of the appearances. It would be quite different if the beings in the world as things in themselves existed *in time*, since in that case the creator of substance would be at the same time the author of the whole mechanism of this substance.

Of so great importance is the separation of time (as well as space) from the existence of things in themselves which was effected in the Critique of the Pure Speculative Reason.

It may be said that the solution here proposed involves great difficulty in itself, and is scarcely susceptible of a lucid exposition. But is any other solution that has been attempted, or that may be attempted, easier and more intelligible? Rather might we say that the dogmatic teachers of metaphysics have shown more shrewdness than candour in keeping this difficult point out of sight as much as possible, in the hope that if they said nothing about it, probably no one would think of it. If science is to be advanced, all difficulties must be *laid open*, and we must even search for those that are hidden, for every difficulty calls forth a remedy, which cannot be discovered without science gaining either in extent or in exactness; and thus even obstacles become means of increasing the thoroughness of science. On the other hand, if the difficulties are intentionally concealed, or merely removed by palliatives, then sooner or later they burst out into incurable mischiefs, which bring science to ruin in an absolute scepticism.

Since it is, properly speaking, the notion of freedom

alone amongst all the ideas of pure speculative reason that so greatly enlarges our knowledge in the sphere of the supersensible, though only of our practical knowledge, I ask myself *why it exclusively possesses so great fertility*, whereas the others only designate the vacant space for possible beings of the pure understanding, but are unable by any means to define the concept of them. I presently find that as I cannot think anything without a category, I must first look for a category for the Rational Idea of freedom with which I am now concerned; and this is the category of *causality*; and although freedom, a *concept of the reason*, being a transcendent concept, cannot have any intuition corresponding to it, yet the *concept of the understanding*—for the synthesis of which the *former* demands the unconditioned—(namely, the concept of causality) must have a sensible intuition given, by which first its objective really is assured. Now, the categories are all divided into two classes—the *mathematical*, which concern the unity of synthesis in the conception of objects, and the *dynamical*, which refer to the unity of synthesis in the conception of the existence of objects. The former (those of magnitude and quality) always contain a synthesis of the *homogeneous*; and it is not possible to find in this the unconditioned antecedent to what is given in sensible intuition as conditioned in space and time, as this would itself have to belong to space and time, and therefore be again still conditioned. Whence it resulted in the Dialectic of Pure Theoretic Reason that the opposite methods of attaining the unconditioned and the totality of the conditions were both wrong. The categories of the second class (those of causality and of the necessity of a thing) did not require this homogeneity (of the conditioned and the condition in the synthesis), since here what we have to explain is not how the intuition is compounded from a manifold in it, but only how the existence of the conditioned object corresponding to it is added to the existence of the condition (added, namely, in the understanding as connected therewith); and in that case it was allowable to suppose in the supersensible world the unconditioned antecedent to the altogether conditioned in the world of sense (both as regards the causal connection and the contingent existence of things themselves), although this unconditioned remained indeterminate, and to make the synthesis transcendent. Hence, it was found in the Dialectic of the Pure Speculative Reason that the two apparently opposite methods of obtaining for the conditioned the unconditioned were not really contradictory, *e.g.* in the synthesis of causality to conceive for the conditioned in the series of causes and effects of the sensible world, a causality which has no sensible condition, and that the same action which, as belonging to the world of sense, is always sensibly conditioned, that is, mechanically necessary, yet at the same time may be derived from a causality not sensibly conditioned—being the causality of the acting being as belonging to the supersensible world—and may consequently be conceived as free. Now, the only point in question was to change this *may be* into *is*; that is, that we should be able to show in an actual case, as it were by a fact, that certain actions imply such a causality (namely, the intellectual, sensibly unconditioned), whether they are actual or only commanded, that is objectively necessary in a practical sense. We could not hope to find this connection in actions actually given in experience as events of the sensible world, since causality with freedom must always be sought outside the world of sense in the world of intelligence. But things of sense are the only things offered to our perception and observation. Hence, nothing remained but to find an incontestable objective principle of causality which excludes all sensible conditions; that is, a principle in which reason does not appeal further to something *else* as a determining ground of its causality, but contains this determining ground itself by means of that principle, and in which therefore it is itself as *pure reason* practical. Now, this principle had not to be searched for or discovered; it had long been in the reason of all men, and incorporated in their nature, and is the principle of *morality*. Therefore, that unconditioned causality, with the faculty of its, namely, freedom, is no longer merely indefinitely and problematically *thought* (this speculative reason could prove to be feasible), but is even *as regards the law of its causality* definitely and assertorially *known*; and with it the fact that a being (I myself) belonging to the world of sense, belongs also to the supersensible world, this is also positively *known*, and thus the reality of the supersensible world is established, and in practical respects *definitely* given, and this definiteness, which for theoretical purposes would be *transcendent*, is for practical purposes *immanent*. We could not, however, make a similar step as regards the second dynamical idea, namely, that of a *necessary being.* We could not rise to it from the sensible world without the aid of the first dynamical idea. For if we attempted to do so, we should have ventured to leave at a bound all that is given to us, and to leap to that of which nothing is given us that can help us to effect the connection of such a supersensible being with the world of sense (since the necessary being would have to be known as given *outside ourselves*). On the other hand, it is now obvious that this connection is quite possible in relation to *our own* subjects, inasmuch as I know myself to be *on the one side* as an intelligible [supersensible] being determined by moral law (by mean of freedom), and on the other side as acting in the world of sense. It is the concept of freedom alone that enables us to find the unconditioned and intelligible (supersensible) for conditioned and sensible without going out of ourselves. For it is our own reason that by means of the supreme and unconditional practical law knows that itself and the being that is conscious of this law (our own person) belongs to the pure world of understanding, and moreover defines the manner in which, as such, it can be active. In this way it can be understood why in the whole faculty of reason it is *the practical reason only* that can help us to pass beyond the world of sense, and give us knowledge of a supersensible order and connection, which, however, for this very reason cannot be extended further than is necessary for pure practical purposes.

Let me be permitted on this occasion to make one more remark, namely, that every step that we make with pure reason, even in the practical sphere where no attention is paid to subtle speculation, nevertheless accords with all the material points of the Critique of the Theoretical Reason as closely and directly as if each step had been thought out with deliberate purpose to establish this confirmation. Such a thorough agreement, wholly unsought for, and quite obvious (as anyone can convince himself, if he will only carry moral enquiries up to their principles), between the most important proposition of practical reason, and the often seemingly too subtle and needless remarks of the Critique of the Speculative Reason, occasions surprise and astonishment, and confirms the maxim already recognized and praised by others, namely, that in every scientific enquiry we should pursue our way steadily with all possible exactness and frankness, without caring for any objection that may be raised from outside its sphere, but, as far as we can, to carry out our enquiry truthfully and completely by itself. Frequent observation has convinced me that when such researches are concluded, that which in one part of them appeared to me very questionable, considered in relation to other extraneous doctrines, when I left this doubtfulness out of sight for a time, and only attended to the business in hand until it was completed, at last was unexpectedly found to agree perfectly with what had been discovered separately without the least regard to those doctrines, and without any partiality or prejudice for them. Authors would save themselves many errors and much labour lost (because spent on a delusion) if they could only resolve to go to work with more frankness.

Of the postulates of pure practical reason in general

They all proceed from the principle of morality, which is not a postulate but a law, by which reason determines the will directly, which will, because it is so determined as a pure will, requires these necessary conditions of obedience to its precept. These postulates are not theoretical dogmas, but suppositions practically necessary; while then they do (not) extend our speculative knowledge, they give objective reality to the ideas of speculative reason in general (by means of their reference to what is practical), and give it a right to concepts, the possibility even of which it could and otherwise venture to affirm.

These postulates are those of *immortality*, *freedom* positively considered (as the causality of a being so far as he belongs to the intelligible world), and the *existence of God*. The *first* results from the practically necessary condition of a duration adequate to the complete fulfilment of the moral law; the *second* from the necessary supposition of independence on the sensible world, and of the faculty of determining one's will according to the law of an intelligible world, that is, of freedom; the third from the necessary condition of the existence of the *summum bonum* in such an intelligible world, by the supposition of the supreme independent good, that is, the existence of God.

Thus the fact that respect for the moral law necessarily makes the *summum bonum* an object of our endeavours, and the supposition thence resulting of its objective reality, lead through the postulates of practical reason to conceptions which speculative reason might indeed present as problems, but could never solve. Thus it leads (1) To that one in the solution of which the latter could do nothing but commit *paralogisms* (namely, that of immortality), because it could not lay hold of the character of permanence, by which to complete the psychological conception of an ultimate subject necessarily ascribed to the soul in self-consciousness, so as to make it the real conception of a substitute, a character which practical reason furnishes by the postulate of a duration required for accordance with the moral law in the *summum bonum*, which is the whole end of practical reason. (2) it leads to that of which speculative reason contained nothing but *antinomy*, the solution of which it could only found on a notion problematically conceivable indeed, but whose objective reality it could not prove or determine, namely, the *cosmological* idea of an intelligible world and the consciousness of our existence in it, by means of the postulate of freedom (the reality of which it lays down by virtue of the moral law), and with it likewise the law of an intelligible world, to which speculative reason could only point, but could not define its conception. (3) What speculative reason was obliged to leave undetermined as a mere transcendental *ideal*, viz. the *theological* conception of the First Being, to this it gives significance (in a practical view, that is, as a condition of the possibility of the object of a will determined by that law), namely as the supreme principle of the *summum bonum* in an intelligible world, by means of moral legislation in it invested with sovereign power.

Is our knowledge, however, actually extended in this way by pure practical reason, and is that *immanent* in practical reason which for the speculative was only *transcendent*? Certainly, but *only in a practical point of view*. For we do not thereby take knowledge of the nature of our souls, nor of the intelligible world, nor of the Supreme Being, with respect to what they are in themselves, but we have merely combined the conceptions of them in the *practical* concept of the *summum bonum* as the object of our will, and this altogether *a priori* but only by means of the moral law, and merely in reference to it, in respect of the object which it commands. But how freedom is possible, and how we are to conceive this kind of causality theoretically and positively, is not thereby discovered; but only that there is such a causality is postulated by the moral law and in its behoof. It is the same with the remaining ideas, the possibility of which no human intelligence will ever fathom, but the truth of which, on the other hand, no sophistry will ever wrest from the conviction even of the commonest man.

Of belief from a requirement of pure reason

A want of requirement of pure reason in its speculative use leads only to *hypothesis*; that of pure practical reason to a *postulate*; for in the former case I ascend from the result as high as I please in the series of causes, not in order to give objective reality to the result (*e.g.* the causal connection of things and changes in the world), but in order thoroughly to satisfy my enquiring reason in respect of it. Thus I see before me order and design in nature, and need not resort to speculation to assure myself of their *reality*, but to *explain* them I have to *presuppose a Deity* as their cause; and then since the inference from an effect to a definite cause is always uncertain and doubtful, especially to a cause so precise and so perfectly defined as we have to conceive in God, hence the highest degree of certainty to which this presupposition can be brought is, that it is the most rational opinion for us men. On the other hand, a requirement of pure *practical* reason is based on a *duty*, that of making something (the *summum bonum*) the object of my will so as to promote it with all my powers; in which case I must suppose its possibility, and consequently also the conditions necessary thereto, namely, God, freedom, and immortality; since I cannot prove these by my speculative reason, although neither can I refute them. This duty is founded on something that is indeed quite independent on these suppositions, and is of itself apodictically certain, namely, the moral law; and so far it needs no further support by theoretical views as to the inner constitution of things, the secret final aim of the order of the world, or a presiding ruler thereof, in order to bind me in the most perfect manner to act in unconditional conformity to the law. But the subjective effect of this law, namely, the mental *disposition* conformed to it and made necessary by it, to promote the practically possible *summum bonum*, this presupposes at least that the latter is *possible*, for it would be practically impossible to strive after the object of a conception which at bottom was empty and had no object. Now the above-mentioned postulates concern only the physical or metaphysical conditions of the *possibility* of the *summum bouum*; in a word, those which lie in the nature of things, not, however, for the sake of an arbitrary speculative purpose, but of practically necessary end of a pure rational will, which in this case does not *choose*, but *obeys* an inexorable command of reason, the foundation of which is *objective*, in the constitution of things as they must be universally judged by pure reason, and is not based on *inclination*; for we are in no-wise justified in assuming, on account of what we *wish* on merely *subjective* grounds, that the means thereto are possible or that its object is real. This, then, is an absolutely necessary requirement, and what it presupposes is not merely justified as an allowable hypothesis, but as a postulate in a practical point of view; and admitting that the pure moral law inexorably binds every man as a command (not as a rule of prudence), the righteous man may say: I *will* that there be a God, that my existence in this world be also an existence outside the chain of physical causes, and in a pure world of the understanding; and lastly, that my duration be endless; I firmly abide by this, and will not let this faith be taken from me; for in this instance alone my interest, because I *must* not relex anything of it, inevitably determines my judgement, without regarding sophistries, however unable I may be to answer them or to oppose them with others more plausible.

In order to prevent misconception in the use of a notion as yet so unusual as that of a faith of pure practical reason, let me be permitted to add one more remark. It might almost seem as if this rational faith were here announced as itself a *command*, namely, that we should assume the *summum bonum* as possible. But a faith that is commanded is nonsense. Let the preceding analysis, however, be remembered of what is required to be supposed in the conception of the *summun bonum*, and it will be seen that it cannot be commanded to assume this possibility, and no practical disposition of mind is required to *admit* it; but that speculative reason must concede it without being asked, for no one can affirm that it is *impossible* in itself that rational beings in the world should at the same time be worthy of happiness and conformity with the moral law, and also possess this happiness proportionately. Now in respect to the first element of the *summum bonum*, namely, that which concerns morality, the moral law gives merely a command, and to doubt the possibility of that element would be the same as to call in question the moral law itself. But as regards the second element of that object, namely, happiness perfectly proportioned to that worthiness, it is true that there is no need of a command to admit its possibility in general, for theoretical reason has nothing to say against it; but *the manner* in which we have to conceive this harmony of the laws of nature with those of freedom has in it something in respect of which we have a *choice*, because theoretical reason decides nothing with apodictic certainty about it, and in respect of this there may be a moral interest which turns the scale.

I had said above that in a mere course of nature in the world an accurate correspondence between happiness and moral worth is not to be expected, and must be regarded as impossible and that therefore the possibility of the *summum bonum* cannot be admitted from this side except on the supposition of a moral Author of the world. I purposely reserved the restriction of this judgment of the *subjective* conditions of our reason, in order not to make use of it until the manner of this belief should be defined more precisely. The fact is that the impossibility referred to is *merely subjective*, that is, our reason finds it *impossible for it* to render conceivable in the way of a mere course of nature a connection so exactly proportioned and so thoroughly adapted to an end, between two sets of events happening according to such distinct laws; although, as with everything else in nature that is adapted to an end, it cannot prove, that is, show by sufficient objective reasons, that it is not possible by universal laws of nature.

Now, however, a deciding principle of a different kind comes into play to turn the scale in this uncertainty of speculative reason. The command to promote the *summum bonum* is established on an objective basis (in practical reason); the possibility of the same in general is likewise established on an objective basis (in theoretical reason, which has nothing to say against it). But reason cannot decide objectively in what way we are to conceive this possibility; whether by universal laws of nature without a wise Author presiding over nature, or only on supposition of such an Author. Now here there comes in a *subjective* condition of reason; the only way theoretically possible for it, of conceiving the exact harmony of the kingdom of nature with the kingdom of morals, which is the condition of the possibility of the *summum bonum*; and at the same time the only conducive to morality (which depends on an objective law of reason). Now since the promotion of this *summum bonum*, and therefore the supposition of its possibility are *objectively* necessary (though only as a result of practical reason), while at the same time the manner in which we would conceive it rests with our own choice, and in this choice a free interest of pure practical reason decides for the assumption of a wise Author of the world; it is clear that the principle that herein determines our judgment, though as a want it is subjective, yet at the same time being the means of promoting what is *objectively* (practically) necessary, is the foundation of a maxim of belief in a moral point of view, that is, a *faith of pure practical reason*. This, then, is not commanded, but being a voluntary determination of our judgment, conducive to the moral (commanded) purpose, and moreover harmonizing with the theoretical requirement of reason, to assume that existence and to make it the foundation of our further employment of reason, it has itself sprung from the moral disposition of mind; it may therefore at times waver even in the well-disposed, but can never be reduced to unbelief.

Religion within the Limits of Reason alone

Concerning the restoration to its power of the original predisposition to good

...From this it follows that man's moral growth of necessity begins not in the improvement of his practices but rather in the transforming of his cast of mind and in the grounding of a character; though customarily man goes about the matter otherwise and fights against vices one by one, leaving undisturbed their common root. And yet even the man of greatest limitations is capable of being impressed by respect for an action conforming to duty— a respect which is the greater the more he isolates it, in thought, from other incentives which, through self-love, might influence the maxim of conduct. Even children are capable of detecting the smallest trace of admixture of improper incentives; for an action thus motivated at once loses, in their eyes, all moral worth. This predisposition to goodness is cultivated in no better way than by adducing the actual *example* of good men (of that which concerns their conformity to law) and by allowing young students of morals to judge the impurity of various maxims on the basis of the actual incentives motivating the conduct of these good men. The predisposition is thus gradually transformed into a cast of mind, and *duty*, for its own sake, begins to have a noticeable importance in their hearts. But to teach a pupil to *admire* virtuous actions, however great the sacrifice these may have entailed, is not in harmony with preserving his feeling for moral goodness. For be a man never so virtuous, all the goodness he can ever perform is still his simple duty; and to do his duty is nothing more than to do what is in the common moral order and hence in no way deserving of wonder. Such wonder is rather a lowering of our feeling for duty, as if to act in obedience to it were something extraordinary and meritorious.

Yet there is one thing in our soul which we cannot cease from regarding with the highest wonder, when we view it properly, and for which admiration is not only legitimate but even exalting, and that is the original moral predisposition itself in us. What is it in us (we can ask ourselves) whereby we, beings ever dependent upon nature through so many needs are, at the same time raised so far above these needs by the idea of an original predisposition (in us) that we count them all as nothing, and ourselves as unworthy of existence, if we cater to their satisfaction (though this alone can make life worth desiring) in opposition to the law—a law by virtue of which our reason commands us potently, yet without making either promises or threats? The force of this question every man, even one of the meanest capacity, must feel most deeply—every man, that is, who previously has been taught the holiness which inheres in the idea of duty but who has not yet advanced to an enquiry into the concept of freedom, which first and foremost emerges from this law: and the very incomprehensibility of this predisposition, which announces a divine origin, acts perforce upon the spirit even to the point of exaltation, and strengthens it for whatever sacrifice a man's respect for his duty may demand of him. More frequently to excite in man this feeling of the dignity of his moral destiny is especially commendable as a method of awakening moral sentiments. For to do so works directly against the innate propensity to invert the incentives in the maxims of our will and toward the re-establishment in the human heart, in the form of an unconditioned respect for the law as the ultimate condition upon which maxims are to be adopted, of the original moral order among the incentives, and so of the predisposition to good in all its purity.

The idea of a people of god can be realized (through human organization) only in the form of a church

The sublime, yet never wholly attainable, idea of an ethical commonwealth dwindles markedly under men's hands. It becomes an institution which, at best capable of representing only the pure form of such a commonwealth, is, by the conditions of sensuous human nature, greatly circumscribed in its means for establishing such a whole.

How indeed can one expect something perfectly straight to be framed out of such crooked wood?

To found a moral people of God is therefore a task whose consummation can be looked for not from men but only from God Himself. Yet man is not entitled on this account to be idle in this business and to let Providence rule, as though each could apply himself exclusively to his own private moral affairs and relinquish to a higher wisdom all the affairs of the human race (as regards its moral destiny). Rather must man proceed as though everything depended upon him; only on this condition dare he hope that higher wisdom will grant the completion of his well-intentioned endeavours.

The wish of all well-disposed people is, therefore, "that the kingdom of God come, that His will be done on earth." But what preparations must they now make that it shall come to pass?

An ethical commonwealth under divine moral legislation is a *church* which, so far as it is not an object of possible experience, is called the *church invisible* (a mere idea serving all as the archetype of what is to be established by men). The *visible church* is the actual union of men into a whole, which harmonizes with that ideal. So far as each separate society maintains, under public laws, an order among its members (in the relation of those who obey its laws to those who direct their obedience), the group, united into a whole (the church) is a *congregation* under authorities, who (called teacher or shepherds of souls) merely administer the affairs of the invisible supreme head thereof. In this function they are called servants of the church, just as, in the political commonwealth, the visible overlord occasionally calls himself the highest servant of the state even though he recognizes no single individual over him (and ordinarily not even the people as a whole). The true (visible) church is that which exhibits the (moral) kingdom of God on earth so far as it can be brought to pass by men. The requirements upon, and hence the tokens of, the true church are the following:

1. *Universality*, and hence its numerical oneness; for which it must possess this characteristic, that, although divided and at variance in unessential opinions, it is none the less, with respect to its fundamental intention, founded upon such basic principles as must necessarily lead to a general unification in a single church (thus, no sectarian divisions).
2. Its *nature* (quality); *i.e. purity*, union under no motivating forces other than *moral* ones (purified of the stupidity of superstition and the madness of fanaticism).
3. Its *relation* under the principle of *freedom*; both the internal relation of its members to one another, and the external relation of the church to political power—both relations as in a *republic* (hence neither a *hierarchy*, nor an *illuminatism*, which is a kind of *democracy* through special inspiration, where the inspiration of one man can differ from that of another, according to the whim of each).

4. Its *modality*, the *unchangeableness* of its *constitution*, yet with the reservation that incidental regulations, concerning merely its *administration*, may be changed according to time and circumstance; to this end, however, it must already contain within itself *a priori* (in the idea of its purpose) settled principles.(Thus [it operates] under primordial laws, once [for all] laid down, as it were out of a book of laws, for guidance; not under arbitrary symbols which, since they lack authenticity, are fortuitous exposed to contradiction, and changeable.)

An ethical commonwealth, then in the form of a church, *i.e.*, as a mere representative of a city of God, really has, as regards its basic principles, nothing resembling a political constitution. For its constitution is neither *monarchical* (under a pope or patriarch), nor *aristocratic* (under bishops and prelates), nor *democratic* (as of sectarian *illuminati*). It could best of all be likened to that of a household (family) under a common, though invisible, moral Father, whose holy Son, knowing His will and yet standing in blood relation with all members of the household, takes His place in making His will better known to them; these accordingly honour the Father in Him and so enter with one another into a voluntary, universal, and enduring union of hearts.

Critique of Judgment

The judgment of taste is aesthetical

In order to decide whether anything is beautiful or not, we refer the representation, not by the understanding to the object for cognition but, by the imagination (perhaps in conjunction with the understanding) to the subject, and its feeling of pleasure or pain. The judgment of taste is therefore not a judgment of cognition, and is consequently not logical but aesthetical, by which we understand that whose determining ground can be *no other than subjective*. Every reference of representations, even that of sensations, may be objective (and then it signifies the real in an empirical representation); save only the reference to the feeling of pleasure and pain, by which noting in the object is signified, but through which there is a feeling in the subject, as it is affected by the representation.

To apprehend a regular purposive building by means of one's cognitive faculty (whether in a clear or a confused way of representation) is something quite different from being conscious of this representation as connected with the sensation of satisfaction. Here the representation is altogether referred to the subject and to its feeling of life, under the name of the feeling of pleasure or pain. This establishes a quite separate faculty of distinction and of judgment, adding nothing to cognition, but only comparing the given representation in the subject with the whole faculty of representation, of which the mind is conscious in the feeling of its state. Given representations in a judgment can be empirical (consequently, aesthetical); but the judgment which is formed by means of them is logical, provided they are referred in the judgment to the object. Conversely, if the given representations are rational, but are referred in a judgment simply to the subject (to its feeling), the judgment is so far always aesthetical.

The satisfaction which determines the judgment of taste is disinterested

The satisfaction which we combine with the representation of the existence of an object is called interest. Such satisfaction always has reference to the faculty of desire, either as its determining ground or as necessarily connected with its determining ground. Now when the question is if a thing is beautiful, we do not want to know whether anything depends or can depend on the existence of the thing either for myself or for anyone else, but how we judge it by mere observation (intuition or reflection). If anyone asks me if I find that palace beautiful which I see before me, I may answer: I do not like things of that kind which are made merely to be stared at. Or I can answer like that Iroquois *sachem* who was pleased in Paris by nothing more than by the cook-shops. Or again after the manner of *Rousseau* I may rebuke the vanity of the great who waste the sweat of the people on such superfluous things. In fine I could easily convince myself that if I found myself on an uninhabited island without the hope of ever again coming among men, and could conjure up just such a splendid building by my mere wish, I should not even give myself the trouble if I had a sufficiently comfortable hut. This may all be admitted and approved; but we are not now talking of this. We wish only to know if this mere representation of the object is accompanied in me with satisfaction, however indifferent I may be as regards the existence of the object of this representation. We easily see that in saying it is *beautiful* and in showing that I have taste, I am concerned, not with that in which I depend on the existence of the object, but with that which I make out of this representation in myself. Everyone must admit that a judgment about beauty, in which the least interest mingles, is very partial and is not a pure judgment of taste. We must not be in the least prejudiced in favour of the existence of things, but be quite indifferent in this respect, in order to play the judge in things of taste.

We cannot, however, better elucidate this proposition which is of capital importance, than by contrasting the pure disinterested[1] satisfaction in judgments of taste, with that which is bound up with an interest, especially if we can at the same time be certain that there are no other kinds of interest than those which are now to be specified.

The beautiful is that which apart from concepts is represented as the object of a universal satisfaction

This explanation of the beautiful can be derived from the preceding explanation of it as the object of an entirely disinterested satisfaction. For the fact of which everyone is conscious, that the satisfaction is for him quite disinterested, implies in his judgment a ground of satisfaction for everyone. For since it does not rest on any inclination of the subject (nor upon any other premeditated interest), but since he who judges feels himself quite *free* as regards the satisfaction which he attaches to the object, he cannot find the ground of this satisfaction in any private conditions connected with his own subject; and hence it must be regarded as grounded on what he can presuppose in every other man. Consequently he must believe that he has reason for attributing a similar satisfaction to everyone. He will

---

1. A judgment upon an object of satisfaction may be quite *disinterested*, but yet very *interesting*, *i.e.* not based upon and interest, but bringing an interest with it; of this kind are all pure moral judgments. Judgments of taste, however, do not in themselves establish any interest. Only in society is it *interesting* to have taste: the reason of this will be shown in the sequel.

therefore speak of the beautiful, as if beauty were a characteristic of the object and the judgment logical (constituting a cognition of the object by means of concepts of it); although it is only aesthetical and involves merely a reference of the representation of the object to the subject. For it has this similarity to a logical judgment that we can presuppose its validity for everyone. But this universality cannot arise from concepts; for from concepts there is no transition to the feeling of pleasure or pain (except in pure practical laws, which bring an interest with them such as is not bound up with the pure judgment of taste). Consequently the judgment of taste, accompanied with the consciousness of separation from all interest, must claim validity for everyone, without this universality depending on objects. That is, there must be bound up with it a title to subjective universality.

Comparison of the beautiful with the pleasant and the good by means of the above characteristic

As regards the present everyone is content that his judgment, which he bases upon private feeling, and by which he says of an object that it pleases him, should be limited merely to his own person. Thus he is quite contented if he says "Canary wine is pleasant," another man may correct his expression and remind him that he ought to say "It is pleasant to *me*" And this is the case not only as regards the taste of the tongue, the palate, and the throat, but for whatever is pleasant to anyone's eyes and ears. To one violet colour is soft and lovely, to another it is faded and dead. One man likes the tone of the wind instruments, another that of strings. To strive here with the design of reproving as incorrect another man's judgment which is different from our own, as if the judgments were logically opposed, would be folly. As regards the pleasant therefore the fundamental proposition is valid, *everyone has his own taste* (the taste of sense).

The case is quite different with the beautiful. It would (on the contrary) be laughable if a man who imagined anything to his own taste, thought to justify himself by saying: "This object (the house we see, the coat that person wears, the concert we hear, the poem submitted to our judgment) is beautiful *for me*." For he must not call it *beautiful* if it merely pleases himself. Many things may have for him charm and pleasantness. No one troubles himself at that; but if he gives out anything as beautiful, he supposes in others the same satisfaction—he judges not merely for himself, but for everyone, and speaks of beauty as if it were a property of things. Hence he says "the *thing* is beautiful"; and he does not count on the agreement of others with this his judgment of satisfaction, because he has found this agreement several times before, but he *demands* it of them. He blames them if they judge otherwise and he denies them taste, which he nevertheless require from them. Here then we cannot say that each man has his own particular taste. For this would be as much as to say that there is no taste whatever; *i.e.* no aesthetical judgment, which can make a rightful claim upon everyone's assent.

At the same time we find as regards the pleasant that there is an agreement among men in the judgments upon it, in regard to which we deny taste to some and attribute it to others; by this not meaning one of our organic senses, but a faculty of judging in respect of the pleasant generally. Thus we say of a man who knows how to entertain his guests with pleasures (of enjoyment for all the senses), so that they are all pleased, "he has taste." But here the universality is only taken comparatively; and there emerged rules which are only *general* (like all empirical ones), and not *universal;* which latter the judgment of Taste upon the beautiful undertakes or lays claim to. It is a judgment in reference to sociability, so far as this rests on empirical rules. In respect of the good it is true that judgments make rightful claim to validity for everyone; but the good is represented only *by means of a concept* as the object of a universal satisfaction, which is the case neither with the pleasant nor with the beautiful.

Have we ground for presupposing a common sense?

Cognitions and judgments must, along with the conviction that accompanies them, admit of universal communicability; for otherwise there would be no harmony between them and the object, and they would be collectively a mere subjective play of the representative powers, exactly as scepticism would have it. But if congnitions are to admit of communicability, so must also the state of mind—*i.e.* the accordance of the cognitive powers with a cognition generally, and that proportion of them which is suitable for a representation (by which an object is given to us) in order that a cognition may be made out of it—admit of universal communicability. For without this as the subjective condition of cognition, knowledge as an effect could not arise. This actually always takes place when a given object by means of sense excites the imagination to collect the manifold, and the imagination in its turn excites the understanding to bring about a unity in this collective process in concepts. But this accordance of the cognitive powers has a different proportion according to the variety of the objects which are given. However, it must be such that this internal relation, by which one mental faculty is excited by another, shall be generally the most beneficial for both faculties in respect of cognition (of given objects); and this accordance can only be determined by feeling (not according to concepts). Since now this accordance itself must admit of universal communicability, and consequently also our feeling of it (in a given representation), and since the universal communicability of a feeling presupposes a common sense, we have grounds for assuming this latter. And this common sense is assumed without relying on psychological observations, but simply as the necessary condition of the universal communicability of our knowledge, which is presupposed in every logic and in every principle of knowledge that is not sceptical.

Of the empirical interest in the beautiful

That the judgment of taste by which something is declared beautiful must have no interest *as its determining ground* has been sufficiently established above. But it does not follow that after it has been given as a pure aesthetical judgment, no interest can be combined with it. This combination, however, can only be indirect, *i.e.* taste must first of all be represented as combined with something else, in order that we may unite with the satisfaction of mere reflection upon an object a *pleasure in its existence* (as that wherein all interest consists). For here also in aesthetical judgments what we say in cognitive judgments (of things in general) is valid; *a posse ad esse non valet consequentia.* This something else may be empirical, viz, an inclination proper to human nature, or intellectual, as the property of the will of being capable of *a priori* determination by reason. Both these involve a satisfaction in the presence of an object, and so can lay the foundation for an interest in what has by itself pleased without reference to any interest whatever.

Empirically the beautiful interests only in *society*. If we admit the impulse to society as natural to man, and his fitness for it, and his propension towards it, *i.e. sociability*, as a requisite for man as a being destined for society, and so as a property belonging to *humanity*, we cannot escape from regarding taste as a faculty for judging everything in respect of which we can communicate our *feeling* to all other men, and so as a means of furthering that which everyone's natural inclination desires.

A man abandoned by himself on a desert island would adorn neither his hut nor his person; nor would he seek for flowers, still less would he plant them, in order to adorn himself therewith. It is only in society that it occurs to him to be not merely a man, but a refined man after his kind (the beginning of civilization). For such do we judge him to be who is both inclined and apt to communicate his pleasure to others, and who is not contented with an object if he cannot feel satisfaction in it in common with others. Again, everyone expects and requires from everyone else this reference to universal communication [of pleasure], as it were from an original compact dictated by humanity itself. Thus, doubtless, in the beginning only those things which attracted the senses, *e.g.* colours for painting oneself (roucou among the Carabs and cinnabar among the Iroquois), flowers, mussel shells, beautiful feathers, etc.—but in time beautiful forms also (e.g. *in their* canoes, and clothes, etc.), which bring with them no gratification, or satisfaction of enjoyment—were important in society, and were combined with great interest. Until at last civilization, having reached its highest point, makes out of this almost the main business of refined inclination; and sensations are only regarded as of worth in so far as they can be universally communicated. Here, although the pleasure which everyone has in such an object is inconsiderable and in itself without any marked interest, yet the Idea of its universal communicability increases its worth in an almost infinite degree.

But this interest that indirectly attaches to the beautiful through our inclination to society, and consequently is empirical, is of no importance for us here; because we have only to look to what may have a reference, although only indirectly, to the judgment of taste *a priori*. For if even in this form an interest bound up therewith should discover itself, taste would discover a transition of our judging faculty from sense-enjoyment to moral feeling; and so not only would be the better guided in employing taste purposively, but there would be thus presented a link in the chain of the human faculties *a priori*, on which all legislation must depend. We can only say thus much about the empirical interest in objects of taste and in taste itself. Since it is subservient to inclination, however refined the latter may be, it may easily be confounded with all the inclinations and passions, which attain their greatest variety and highest degree in society; and the interest in the beautiful, if it is grounded thereon, can only furnish a very ambiguous transition from the pleasant to the good. But whether this can or cannot be furthered by taste, taken in its purity, is what we now have to investigate.

Of beauty as the symbol of marality

Intuitions are always required to establish the reality of our concepts. If the concepts are empirical, the intuitions are called *examples*. If they are pure concepts of understanding, the intuitions are called *schemata*. If we desire to establish the objective reality of rational concepts, *i.e.* of ideas, on behalf of theoretical cognition, then we are asking for something impossible, because absolutely no intuition can be given which shall be adequate to them.

All hypotyposis (presentation, *subjectio sub adspectum*), or sensible illustration, is twofold. It is either *schematical*, when to a concept comprehended by the understanding the corresponding intuition is given *a priori*; or it is *symbolical*. In the latter case to a concept only thinkable by the reason, to which no sensible intuition can be adequate, an intuition is supplied with which accords a procedure of the judgment analogous to what it observes in schematism: it accords with it, that is, in respect of the rule of this procedure merely, not of the intuition itself; consequently in respect of the form of reflection merely, and not of its content.

There is a use of the word *symbolical* that has been adopted by modern logicians, which is misleading and incorrect, *i.e.* to speak of the *symbolical* mode of representation as if it were opposed to the *intuitive;* for the symbolical is only a mode of the *intuitive*. The latter (the intuitive), that is, may be divided into the *schematical* and the *symbolical* modes of representation. Both are hypotyposes, *i.e.* presentations (*exhibitiones*); not mere *characterizations*, or designations of concepts by accompanying sensible signs which contain nothing belonging to the intuition of the object, and only serve as a means for reproducing the concepts, according to the law of association of the imagination, and consequently in a subjective point of view. These are either words, or visible (algebraical, even mimetical) signs, as mere expressions for concepts.

All intuitions, which we supply to concepts *a priori*, are therefore either *schemata* or *symbols*, of which the former contain direct, the latter indirect, presentations of the concept. The former do this demonstratively; the latter by means of an analogy (for which we avail ourselves even of empirical intuitions) in which the judgment exercises a double function; first applying the concept to the object of a sensible intuition, and then applying the mere rule of the reflection made upon that intuition to a quite different object of which the first is only the symbol. Thus a monarchical state is represented by a living body, if it is governed by national laws, and by a mere machine (like a hand-mill) if governed by an individual absolute will; but in both cases only *symbolically*. For between a despotic state and a hand-mill there is, to be sure, no similarity; but there is a similarity in the rules according to which we reflect upon these two things and their causality. This matter has not been sufficiently analysed hitherto, for it deserves a deeper investigation; but this is not the place to linger over it. Our language [*i.e.* German] is full of indirect presentations of this sort, in which the expression does not contain the proper scheme for the concept, but merely a symbol for reflection. Thus the words *ground* (support, basis), *to depend* (to be held up from above), to *flow* from something (instead of, to follow), *substance* (as *Locke* expresses it, the support of accidents), and countless others, are not schematical but symbolical hypotyposes and expressions for concepts, not by means of a direct intuition, but only by analogy with it, *i.e.* by the transference of reflection upon an object of intuition to a quite different concept to which perhaps an intuition can never directly correspond. If we are to give the name of cognition to a mere mode of representation (which is quite permissible if the latter is not a principle of the theoretical determination of what an object is in itself, but of the practical determination of what the idea of it should be for us and for its purposive use), then all our knowledge of God is merely symbolical; and he who regards it as schematical, along with the properties of understanding, will, etc., which only establish their objective reality in beings of this world, falls into anthropomorphism, just as he who gives up every intuitive element falls into Deism, by which nothing at all is cognized, not even in a practical point of view.

Now I say the beautiful is the symbol of the morally good, and that it is only in this respect (a reference which is natural to every man and which every man postulates in others as a duty) that it gives pleasure with a claim for the agreement of everyone else. By this the mind is made conscious of a certain ennoblement and elevation above the mere sensibility to pleasure received through sense, and the worth of others is estimated in accordance with a like maxim of their judgment. That is the *intelligible*, to which, as pointed out in the preceding paragraph, taste looks; with which our higher cognitive faculties are in accord; and without which a downright contradiction would arise between their nature and the claims made by taste. In this faculty the judgment does not see itself, as in empirical judging, subjected to a heteronomy of empirical laws; it gives the law to itself in respect of the objects of so pure a satisfaction, just as the reason does in respect of the faculty of desire. Hence, both on account of this inner possibility in the subject and of the external possibility of a nature that agrees with it, it finds itself to be referred to something within the subject as well as without him, something which is neither nature nor freedom, but which yet is connected with the supersensible ground of the latter. In this supersensible ground, therefore, the theoretical faculty is bound together in unity with the practical, in a way which though common is yet unknown. We shall indicate some points of this analogy, while at the same time we shall note the differences.

(1) The beautiful pleases *immediately* (but only in reflective intuition, not, like morality, in its concept). (2) It pleases *apart from any interest* (the morally good is indeed necessarily bound up with an interest, though not with one which precedes the judgment upon the satisfaction, but with one which is first of all produced by it). (3) The *freedom* of the imagination (and therefore of the sensibility of our faculty) is represented in judging the beautiful as harmonious with the conformity to law of the understanding (in the moral judgment the freedom of the will is thought as the harmony of the latter with itself according to universal laws of reason). (4) The subjective principle in judging the beautiful is represented as *universal, i.e.* as valid for every man, though not cognizable through any universal concept. (The objective principle of morality is also expounded as universal, *i.e.* for every subject and for every action of the same subject, and thus as cognizable by means of a universal concept). Hence the moral judgment is not only susceptible of definite constitutive principles, but is possible *only* by grounding its maxims on these in their universality.

A reference to this analogy is usual even with the common understanding [of men], and we often describe beautiful objects of nature or art by names that seem to put a moral appreciation at their basis. We call buildings or trees majestic and magnificent, landscapes laughing and gay; even colours are called innocent, modest, tender, because they excite sensations which have something analogous to the consciousness of the state of mind brought about by moral judgments. Taste makes possible the transition, without any violent leap, from the charm of sense to habitual moral interest; for it represents the imagination in its freedom as capable of purposive determination for the understanding, and so teaches us to find even in objects of sense a free satisfaction apart from any charm of sense.

Things regarded as natural purposes are organized beings

According to the character alleged in the preceding section, a thing, which, though a natural product, is to be cognized as only possible as a natural purpose, must bear itself alternately as cause and as effect. This, however, is a somewhat inexact and indeter-minate expression which needs derivation from a determinate concept.

Causal combination as thought merely by the understanding is a connection constituting an ever-progressive series (of causes and effects); and things which as effects presuppose others as causes cannot be reciprocally at the same time causes of these. This sort of causal combination we call that of effective causes (*nexus effectivus*). But on the other hand, a causal combination according to a concept of reason (of purposes) can also be thought, which regarded as a series would lead either forwards or backwards; in this the thing that has been called the effect may with equal propriety be termed the cause of that of which it is the effect. In the practical department of human art we easily find connections such as this; *e.g.* a house, no doubt, is the cause of the money received for rent, but also conversely the representation of this possible income was the cause of building the house. Such a causal connection we call that of final causes (*nexus finalis*). We may perhaps suitably name the first the connection of real causes, the second of those which are ideal; because from this nomenclature it is at once comprehended that there can be no more than these two kinds of causality.

For a thing to be a natural purpose in the *first* place it is requisite that its parts (as regards their being and their form) are only possible through their reference to the whole. For the thing itself is a purpose and so is comprehended under a concept or an idea which must determine *a priori* all that is to be contained in it. But so far as a thing is only thought as possible in this way, it is a mere work of art; *i.e.* a product of one rational cause distinct from the matter (of the parts), whose causality (in the collection and combination of the parts) is determined through its idea of a whole possible by their means (and consequently not through external nature).

But if a thing as a natural product is to involve in itself and in its internal possibility a reference to purposes—*i.e.* to be possible only as a natural purpose, and without the causality of the concepts of rational beings external to itself—then it is requisite *secondly* that its parts should so combine in the unity of a whole that they are reciprocally cause and effect of each other's form. Only in this way can the idea of the whole conversely (reciprocally) determine the form and combination of all the parts; not indeed as cause—for then it would be an artificial product—but as the ground of cognition, for him who is judging it, of the systematic unity and combination of all the manifold contained in the given material.

For a body then which is to be judged in itself and its internal possibility as a natural purpose, it is requisite that its parts mutually depend upon each other both as to their form and their combination, and so produce a whole by their own causality; while conversely the concept of the whole may be regarded as its cause according to a principle (in a being possessing a causality according to concepts adequate to such a product). In this case then the connection of *effective causes* may be judged as an *effect through final* causes.

In such a product of nature every part not only exists *by means of* the other parts but is thought as existing *for the sake of* the others and the whole, that is, as an (organic) instrument. Thus, however, it might be an artificial instrument, and so might be represented only as a purpose that is possible in general; but also its parts are all organs reciprocally *producing* each other. This can never be the case with artificial instruments, but only with nature which supplies all the material for instruments (even for those of art). Only a product of such a kind can be called a *natural purpose*, and this because it is an *organized* and *self-organizing being*.

In a watch one part is the instrument for moving the other parts, but the wheel is not the effective cause of the production of the others; no doubt one part is for the sake of the others, but it does not exist by their means. In this case the producing cause of the parts and of their form is not contained in the nature (of the material), but is external to it in a being which can produce effects according to ideas of a whole possible by means of its causality. Hence a watch wheel does not produce other wheels, still less does one watch produce other watches, utilizing (organizing) foreign material for that purpose; hence it does not replace of itself parts of which it has been deprived, nor does it makes good what is lacking in a first formation by the addition of the missing parts, nor if it has gone out of repair itself—all of which, on the contrary, we may expect from organized nature. An organized being is then not a mere machine, for that has merely *moving* power, but it possesses in itself *formative* power of a self-propagating kind which it communicates to its materials though they have it not of themselves; it organizes them, in fact, and this cannot be explained by the mere mechanical faculty of motion.

We say of nature and its faculty in organized products far too little if we described it as an *analogon of art;* for this suggests an artificer (a rational being) external to it. Much rather does it organize itself and its organized products in every species, no doubt after one general pattern but yet with suitable deviations, which self-preservation demands according to circumstances. We perhaps approach nearer to this inscrutable property, if we describe it as an *analogon of life;* but then we must either endow matter, as mere matter, with a property which contradicts its very being (hylosoism), or associate therewith an alien principle *standing in communion* with it (a soul). But in the latter case we must, if such a product is to be a natural product, either presuppose organized matter as the instrument of that soul, which does not make the soul a whit more comprehensible; or regard the soul as artificer of this structure and so remove the product from (corporeal) nature. To speak strictly, then, the organization of nature has in it nothing analogous to any causality we know. Beauty in nature can be rightly described as an analogon of art, because it is ascribed to objects only in reference to reflection upon their *external* aspect, and consequently only on account of the form of their external surface. But *internal natural perfection*, as it belongs to those things which are only possible as *natural purposes*, and are therefore called organized beings, is not analogous to any physical, *i.e.* natural, faculty known to us; nay even, regarding ourselves as, in the widest sense, belonging to nature, it is not even thinkable or explicable by means of any exactly fitting analogy to human art.

The concept of a thing as in itself a natural purpose is therefore no constitutive concept of understanding or of reason, but it can serve as a regulative concept for the reflective judgment, to guide our investigation about objects of this kind by a distant analogy with our own causality according to purposes generally, and in our meditations upon their ultimate ground. This latter use, however, is not in reference to the knowledge of nature or of its original ground, but rather to our own practical faculty of reason, in analogy with which we considered the cause of that purposiveness.

Organized beings are then the only beings in nature which, considered in themselves and apart from any relation to other things, can be thought as possible only as purposes of nature. Hence they first afford objective reality to the concept of a purpose of nature, as distinguished from a practical purpose; and so they give to the science of nature the basis for a teleology. *i.e.* a mode of judgment above natural objects according to a special principle which otherwise we should in no way be justified in introducing (because we cannot see *a priori* the possibility of this kind of causality).

The reason that we cannot treat the concept of a technic of nature dogmatically is the fact that a natural purpose is inexplicable.

We deal with a concept dogmatically (even thought it should be empirically conditioned) if we consider it as contained under another concept of the object which constitutes a principle of reason, and determine it in conformity with this. But we deal with it merely critically, if we consider it only in reference to our cognitive faculties and consequently to the subjective conditions of thinking it, without undertaking to decide anything about its object. Dogmatic procedure with a concept is then that which is conformable to law for the determinant judgment, critical procedure for the reflective judgment.

Now the concept of a thing as a natural purpose is a concept which subsumes nature under a causality only thinkable through reason, in order to judge in accordance with this principle about that which is given of the object in experience. But in order to use it dogmatically for the determinant judgment, we must be assured first of the objective reality of this concept, because otherwise we could subsume no natural thing under it. Again, the concept of a thing as a natural purpose is, no doubt, empirically conditioned, *i.e.* only possible under certain conditions given in experience, though not to be abstracted therefrom; but it is a concept only possible in accordance with a rational principle in the judgment about the object. Its objective reality, therefore (*i.e.* that an object in conformity with it is possible), cannot be comprehended and dogmatically established as such a principle; and we do not know whether it is merely a sophistical and objectively empty concept (*conceptus ratiocinans*), or a rational concept, establishing a cognition and confirmed by reason (*conceptus ratiocinatus*). Therefore it cannot be dogmatically treated for the determinant judgment, *i.e.* it is not only impossible to decide whether or not things of nature considered as natural purposes require for their production a causality of a quite peculiar kind (that acting on design); but the question cannot even be put, because the concept of a natural purpose is simply not susceptible of proof through reason as regards its objective reality. That is, it is not constitutive for the determinant judgment, but merely regulative for the reflective.

That it is not susceptible of proof is clear because (as concept of a *natural product*) it embraces in itself natural necessity, and at the same time (as purpose) a contingency of the form of the object (in reference to the mere laws of nature) in the very same thing. Hence, if there is to be no contradiction here it must contain a ground for the possibility of the thing in nature, and also a ground of the possibility of this nature itself and of its reference to something which, not being empirically cognizable nature (supersensible), is therefore for us not cognizable at all. [This is requisite] if it is to be judge according to a different kind of causality from that of natural mechanism when we wish to establish its possibility. The concept of a thing, then, as a natural purpose, is transcendent *for the determinant judgment*, if we consider the object through reason (although for the reflective judgment it certainly may be immanent in respect of the objects of experience). Hence for determinant judgments objective reality cannot be supplied to it; and so it is intelligible how all systems that one may project for the dogmatic treatment of the concept of natural purposes and of nature itself [considered] as a whole connected together by means of final causes, can decide nothing either by objective affirmation or by objective denial. For if things be subsumed under a concept that is merely problematical, its synthetical predicates (*e.g.* in the question whether the purpose of nature which we conceive for the production of things is designed or undersigned) can furnish only problematical judgments of the object, whether affirmative or negative; and we do not know whether we are judging about something or about nothing. The concept of a causality through purposes (of art) has at all events objective reality, and also the concept of a causality according to the mechanism of nature. But the concept of a causality of nature according to the rule of purposes—still more of a Being such as cannot be given us in experience, a Being who is the original cause of nature—thought it can be thought without contradiction, yet is of no avail for dogmatic determinations. For, since it cannot be derived from experience, and also is not requisite for the possibility thereof, its objective reality can in no way be assured. But even it this could be done, how can I number among the products of nature things which are definitely accounted products of divine art, when it is just the incapacity of nature to produce such things according to its own laws that made it necessary to invoke a cause different from it?